So, You N

MW00533302

(Now What?)

Pocket Guide to the
Great Tribulation

Wesley Felter
Harpazo Publishing Company

So, You Missed the Rapture

Published by
Harpazo Publishing Company
Houston, Texas

Copyright 2017 Harpazo Publishing Company

All rights reserved. No part of this book, including interior design, cover design and icons may be reproduced or transmitted in any form, by any means (electronic, photocopying, recording or otherwise) without the prior written permission of the publisher.

ISBN: 978-0-9829954-1-9 (13)

Printed in the United States of America

All Scripture quotes are from the public domain King James Version.

Images from Dreamstime.com and are royalty free.

Wesley Paul Felter; PhD Christian Apologetics, MA Biblical Studies

Back cover Scriptures: Joel 2:1-2, Zephaniah 1:15, Amos 5:20

This book is dedicated to the Lord Jesus Christ. Without the leading and revelation of the Holy Spirit in preparing this work, it would not have been possible.

1 Contents

'Tis not the days of carefree living and marvelous wonder
'Tis not the days of comfort and heavenly bliss

'Tis a time all foolish trivialities come asunder
'Tis a time for righteous living or be damned, eternally amiss!

Mightily, clouds of spiritual armies gather for warfare
One armed with light, the other storms unleashed darkness

Whilst still that thou can see, can hear, can knowest to care
Prepare thee the way back to thy "Maker", urgently with boldness

Harken! O' watchman of thy soul; do take heed!
Warnings of a shaking for the heavens, earth and man abide

Kingdoms and principalities implode with wicked evil deeds
Woes on the horizon, blood moon rises; a blackened sun cannot hide

Wormwood waters, bitterness floods heartless hearts from ponder
Winds of change alarm The Twilight Hour blowing Satan's ominous hiss

'Tis not the days of carefree living and marvelous wonder
'Tis the time for righteous living or be damned, eternally amiss!

AWAKE! O' sleeper, from thy godless dream of unimagined deception
'Cause there will be no peace and security for such a time as this!

Empty, worldly, fleshy attractions, deflect the truth with distraction
Repent!, Repent!, Redeem the NOW!, for what thou seizes forever is!

'Tis not the days of wine and roses!
'Tis a time of blood, thorns and crosses!

The Twilight Hour
Lola Felter (my wonderful wife)
03.16.14

Preface

The purpose of this guide is to give those that miss the Rapture of the Church some detailed information of what lay ahead for them. This is not an academic treatise on Bible prophecy written for scholars. It is a guide written in conversational tone for those that have little or no familiarity with end times Bible prophecy. The vast majority of people on earth will miss the Rapture. Many will be looking for answers. I hope this book finds its way into their hands. By the grace of the Lord Jesus Christ, it will.

If you are familiar with Bible prophecy, then this will be a great refresher as the major prophecy topics are discussed. If you are reading this prior to the Rapture event, then keep it in a safe place as you might need it in the future. If you are sure about your position in Christ, then give this book to one of your friends or loved ones that is not a Christian. Ask them to save it as a resource for when that day comes. Believe me; they are going to need all the help they can get.

1 Introduction

Many will show up for Church the Sunday after the Rapture. They are confused and have many questions. Was it really the Rapture they missed? After all, they are good Christians, right? Then why are we still here they ask. Some will be angry blaming their pastors for not preaching the truths of Bible prophecy and preparing them for so great an event.

Others will show up realizing something very serious has happened but don't know exactly what. They might have heard about the Rapture, but always thought it was just a bizarre delusion of irrational Christians. These folks are probably more

1

open to Jesus than the bunch that has been playing church for decades as they might be realizing all that seemingly inexplicable prophecy just might be true.

As you know, fear of the unknown is a powerful motivator. People do some crazy things when fear rules their mind. Even though things may seem hopeless, all is not lost. I wrote this short guide to help those remaining after the Rapture understand what lay ahead. There are some terrible times coming upon the earth, but if you know about them in advance and prepare, your chances for survival are greatly improved.

This work is a quick survey of the seven-year Tribulation that precedes the Second Coming of Jesus Christ. I cover the major events that occur during this period of distress and tumult. As you read this little book, prepare a chart or journal timeline for the seven years and document what happens on the earth. You can also use the Tribulation Overview chapter to track the events as they occur. This will help you understand the progression of events that lead to the second coming of the Lord Jesus Christ.

Some of the catastrophic events of the Tribulation are local to the Middle East, but many will have a global impact. Don't rely on the main stream American media to report the facts, as they are part and parcel of the corrupt global government-media-corporate system. They will be the source of propaganda and lies, not truth. You think the fake news is bad today, just wait until the seven-year Tribulation begins.

Find an underground or international news source that reports daily on Middle East events. It might be a good idea to get a short-wave receiver and tune in to some international stations. CNN might do a fair job of reporting as they really love being on location when catastrophe strikes, but beware of their analysis of the events.

It grieves me that so many Christians do not study Bible prophecy and are unaware of what is coming upon the earth. They are not looking for the return of Christ for His Church. The Rapture event will find these believers not ready. They will be left behind to endure the seven-year tribulation and many will fall away from the faith. Many others will be martyred for their faith as they stand for Jesus Christ and the truth. Those that have scoffed and mocked Bible prophecy will find themselves living it out.

This guide will warn you of what is coming and how to stand when all hell is breaking loose and great fear has captured the hearts of many. As you read do not skip over the Scriptures in italics. They are the empowered Word of God, everything else is just me.

"And there shall be signs in the sun, and in the moon, and in the stars; and upon the earth distress of nations, with perplexity; the sea and the waves

roaring; **Men's hearts failing them for fear, and for looking after those things which are coming on the earth:** *for the powers of heaven shall be shaken." Luke 21:25-26*

2   Headline News

2.1   - Millions Missing

You awoke one morning to the news that millions of people have simply vanished. People from all walks of life and every country have disappeared virtually into thin air leaving everything behind, even the cloths they were wearing. News networks offer little comfort or explanation for the mass disappearance. Perhaps it was a mass alien abduction and the  missing are on the "mother ship." Maybe they simply stepped into an alternate reality or some parallel universe. Maybe a series of space portals opened and a bunch of folks stepped out into the cosmos.

2.2   - ET Event

Just today I saw an article on Fox News with the headline "Aliens Could Attack Earth to End Global Warming, NASA Scientist Frets." Here are some quotes from the article.

"A team of American researchers have produced a range of scenarios in which aliens could attack the earth, and curiously, one revolves around climate change. They speculate that extraterrestrial environmentalists could be so appalled by our planet-polluting ways that they view us as a threat to the intergalactic ecosystem and decide to destroy us. The thought-provoking scenario is one of many envisaged in a joint study by Penn State and the NASA Planetary Science Division, entitled "Would Contact with Extraterrestrials Benefit or Harm Humanity? A Scenario Analysis." Extraterrestrial intelligence (ETI) "could attack and kill us, enslave us, or potentially even eat us. ETI could attack us out of selfishness or out of a more altruistic desire to protect the galaxy from us. We might be a threat to the galaxy just as we are a threat to our home planet," it warns... It speculates that aliens, worried we might inflict the damage done to our own planet on others, might "seek to preemptively destroy our civilization in order to protect other civilizations from us."

Is this bizarre or what? Mind you, we are not talking about a bunch of wacko UFO freaks that spend their vacations at Roswell. These are PhD scientists at NASA and Penn State University. Mad scientists, I might add. The scientific community and the media are propagandizing viewers to accept mass alien abduction as rationale for the Rapture event. "Extraterrestrial environmentalists"; I

Pocket Guide to the Tribulation

always felt that crowd was a bit strange, now I realize they are aliens. That explains a lot. ☺

2.3 - Who is Missing

All kidding aside, there is a common thread; seems like the missing were all Christians. A few are saying this was the Rapture of the Church taught for centuries by Bible believing Christians. These folks are probably not getting much air time. Others are saying "good riddance", now we can get on with the New World Order. The aliens have done earth a favor; fewer people, less pollution, more food for those remaining, less resources consumed, etc. You get the picture, population reduction, Georgia Guide stones, U. N. Agenda 2030, etc.

Whatever excuses are made for this event, the reality is that millions of real people are really gone. But you are still here. You have, in fact, missed the Rapture of the Church; the catching away of the true believers in Jesus Christ. Let's take a quick look at the concept of the Rapture so you understand what just took place.

Oh, just in case you are concerned about family and friends that were taken, don't worry, they are safely in heaven with the Lord Jesus Christ and will return with Him in seven years. Believe me, they are much better off than you.

3   The Rapture

3.1   - Return for the Bride

The vanished millions are the true believers in the Lord Jesus Christ, referred to as the Bride of Christ. Jesus promised that after He went away He would return for those that believe in Him. He promised that he would return for His followers and take them out of this world to heaven. This catching away of believers living and dead is commonly known as the Rapture.

"Let not your heart be troubled: ye believe in God, believe also in me. In my Father's house are many

*mansions: if [it were] not [so], I would have told you. I
go to prepare a place for you. And if I go and prepare a
place for you,* **I will come again, and receive you
unto myself***; that where I am, [there] ye may be also."
John 14:1-3*

3.2 - Floating in the Clouds

At the Rapture, all true believers in Jesus
Christ dead and alive were gathered to meet the
Lord in the air. Saints who have lived and died for
the past two thousand years were raised from the
dead and the living were all changed, given bodies
fit for heaven, immortal and indestructible. The
event you missed was for true believers in Jesus
and they were the only ones to hear the trumpet
and shout. The Rapture took place in a fraction of a
second, without warning or announcement to the
unbelieving world.

*"For the Lord himself shall descend from
heaven with a shout, with the voice of the archangel,
and with the trump of God: and the dead in Christ shall
rise first:* **Then we which are alive [and] remain
shall be caught up together with them in the
clouds, to meet the Lord in the air: and so shall
we ever be with the Lord**.*" 1 Thessalonians 4:16-17*

*"Behold, I shew you a mystery; We shall not all
sleep, but* **we shall all be changed***, In a moment, in
the twinkling of an eye, at the last trump: for the
trumpet shall sound, and the dead shall be raised*

incorruptible, and we shall be changed." 1 Corinthians
15:51-52

3.3 - The Rapture Effect

The Rapture will have a devastating effect
on the world, especially America. Will the global
elite miss these people especially the poor? Just
that many less mouths to feed in their view. But
millions of hard working, taxpaying Americans are
now permanently gone. Business, military,
government and every other institution has
suffered a tremendous loss of staff, leadership and
expertise. The economy will take a big hit as
monthly tax revenues plummet. Sadly, the greatest
country to ever exist will not be able to recover from
the Rapture. I say this because America in not
mentioned in Bible prophecy. What's coming to the
land of the free and the home of the brave will make
the great depression look like spring break. Get
ready and prepare.

3.4 - Unspeakable Reward

While all hell is breaking loose on earth, the
missing believers are in heaven with the Lord Jesus
Christ enjoying a celebration of unprecedented
happiness, excitement and joy. Believers are also
receiving rewards for their deeds done for Jesus in
accordance with His will and plan for their lives.
Believers are judged for potential reward not
salvation.

"For ***we must all appear before the judgment seat of Christ****; that every one may receive the things [done] in [his] body, according to that he hath done, whether [it be] good or bad." 2 Corinthians 5:10*

"But ***lay up for yourselves treasures in heaven****, where neither moth nor rust doth corrupt, and where thieves do not break through nor steal:" - Matthew 6:20*

3.5   - Your Stuff

Jesus said to lay up treasures in heaven, not on earth. These treasures are now being given to believers and they will never be lost or stolen. Remember, everything on earth is temporal and left behind; only treasures in heaven are eternal. Their home, furniture, cars, bank accounts and 401k's, all left behind, even the junk in the garage. But look at it this way. You have no issues, ills or problems that the Rapture won't immediately fix.   Praise God!

3.6   - What about the Children

The Rapture has separated families and friends. However, children and babies are also gone as they are too young to understand what happened and what is at stake. They will grow up in heaven completely separated from the corruption and pollutions of this world. If you want to see them again you absolutely MUST do what I tell you in the next section.

3.7 - Critical Next Step

The next section is the "(now what?)" part of this guide. You must follow it precisely if there is to be any hope for you. It  explains your eternal destiny, which is far more important than surviving the Tribulation. Your response is far more important than your life on this planet. Where you spend eternity is far more critical than how you fare during the next seven years. As the Knight Templar in Indiana Jones and the Last Crusade said, "choose wisely." It's just that simple.

4 Your Top Priority

4.1 - Top Priority

Since you missed the Rapture, it is obvious that you are not a true follower of Jesus Christ. Oh yes, you may have attended Church on Sunday occasionally, but you never received Jesus Christ as your Lord and Savior. You never truly gave Jesus your life and followed Him. You probably believed in the man Jesus as a great person or moral example. You could have believed that Jesus was a unique historical figure and a great teacher. You could have accepted Jesus intellectually but never repented of your sin and received Him as Savior and Lord of your life.

Well, this is now your **Top** priority. As I will show throughout this writing, receiving Jesus as Lord and Savior will determine whether you receive eternal life with Him or spend eternity in the lake of fire. In the final analysis, there are only two destinations for man; eternal life or eternal damnation. In other words, its heaven or hell, the choice is yours.

*"Marvel not at this: for the hour is coming, in the which all that are in the graves shall hear his voice, And shall come forth; they that have done good, unto the **resurrection of life**; and they that have done evil, unto the **resurrection of damnation**." John 5:28-29*

4.2 - It's Black and White

You can choose life and heaven by receiving Jesus as your Lord and Savior. Or, you can choose hell simply by doing nothing and going along with the world's lies. Believe the media propaganda, follow the Antichrist and your fate in hell is sealed. If that be your choice, then please give this book to someone who desires the truth.

What is the truth? What is the true gospel of Jesus Christ? In a nutshell, the true gospel centers on the death, burial and resurrection of Jesus Christ. Jesus Christ died on the cross and shed His blood as the holy sacrifice for sin. His atoning death on the cross provided the means for you and me to be in right standing with God. Jesus was buried in a fresh tomb showing that he did truly die. Three days later Jesus rose from the dead validating that He truly was and is the Son of God, God in the flesh.

4.3 - The Only Way

I realize that you might be somewhat confused at this point. When this makes sense to you pray a simple prayer like this, "Lord Jesus, I believe you are the Son of the living God, the Savior of the world; I believe you died on the cross for my sin and rose from the dead the third day; I repent of my sin; Cleanse me from all sin by your blood. I give you my life and receive you as my Lord and Savior, Amen." Or, if that is too much then just cry out "HELP ME JESUS." Either way, Jesus knows your heart and will respond to you. If you can find a Bible read the New Testament and the Old Testament prophets. Start your Bible reading with the gospel of John.

*"Jesus answered and said unto him, Verily, verily, I say unto thee, **Except a man be born again**, he cannot see the kingdom of God." John 3:3*

4.4 - Your Testimony

Now that you have given your life to the Lord Jesus Christ, he is your testimony. Your testimony is that you believe in Jesus Christ as your Lord and Savior; He is your King and no other. This

17

is very important as you will need to walk out this testimony over the seven-year Tribulation period. Remember, your eternal destiny is at stake, we are not playing church. This is not about joining a religion. It's about a personal relationship with Jesus Christ that determines your eternal home.

*"And they overcame him (antichrist) by the **blood of the Lamb** (Jesus), and by the **word of their testimony**; and they loved not their lives unto the death." Revelation 12:11 parenthesis mine*

"But he that shall endure unto the end, the same shall be saved." Matthew 24:13

This testimony of Jesus Christ will cost many their lives as you have read above. Better to die for Jesus and go to heaven, than to renounce Him and be cast into hell. You will only overcome, by the blood of Jesus and the word of your testimony. Jesus said:

*"For whosoever will **save** his life[to himself] shall **lose** it: and whosoever will **lose** his life for my sake shall find it." Matthew 16:25 emphasis mine*

I realize this is pretty heavy stuff, but you are living in pretty heavy times and this is the most serious decision you will ever make. Ok, I think you get the point, but I will talk more about this as we proceed.

4.5 - Modern Pastors

If you are a church goer and your pastor did not preach on Bible topics like sin, repentance, being born again and the second coming of Jesus, then next Sunday ask him why. Ask him why he did not preach the true Gospel of Jesus Christ and His Second Coming prophecies. After all, had he preached the truth, you might have gone in the Rapture and would not need to endure the coming seven-year Tribulation.

Let him know his judgment will be severe for not preaching the truth of the Word of God. If he tries to make excuses instead of repenting, leave and find a group of true believers. The Apostle Paul stated in his letter to Timothy:

*"Now the Spirit speaketh expressly, that **in the latter times some shall depart from the faith**, giving heed to seducing spirits, and doctrines of devils."*

4.6 - Like Minded People

Be sure you associate yourself with a group that stresses the truth of God's Word, the Bible. The Word of God is your only source of truth for these last days. Study the prophetic scriptures as they are unfolding right before your very eyes.

Deception and lies are the order of the day for those clinging to the world for answers. Separate yourself from them and cling to the Word of God and the Lord Jesus Christ. Oh, forget about the modern Bible translations, get a King James Version because the prophetic scriptures are easier to follow and the textual links are much clearer making it easier to reference similar verses. If you are new to the Bible, then study the Gospel of John and the New Testament. When you feel comfortable with that then study the prophetic Scriptures found throughout this book. Your increased understanding of coming end times events will give you confidence in the Lord when the hearts of others are failing for fear. Keep the faith in love.

"Watch ye therefore, and pray always, that ye may be **accounted worthy to escape** *all these things that shall come to pass, and to stand before the Son of man." Luke 21:36*

After all is said and done, it is better to be a doorman in God's Kingdom than to reign with the wicked.

"For a day in thy courts [is] better than a thousand (elsewhere). I had rather be a doorkeeper in the house of my God, than to dwell in the tents of wickedness." Psalm 84:10 Parenthesis mine

5   The Tribulation

5.1   - Peace and Security

The seven year "Tribulation" begins with a seven-year major peace treaty being confirmed in the Middle East and ends with the second coming of Jesus Christ. This seven-year period begins shortly after the Rapture of the Church. If you missed the Rapture, then the seven-year Tribulation has probably already begun. In the Old Testament of the Bible this period is called the "Day of the Lord." This is the most horrific seven years the earth will ever know.

*"For when they shall say, **Peace and safety**; then **sudden destruction** cometh upon them"* - 1 Thessalonians 5:3 KJV

5.2 - Unrestrained Evil

This seven-year Tribulation period is the culmination of the age we have been living in since Jesus walked on the earth. During this seven-year Tribulation God's restraint of evil is removed. The restrainer of diabolical evil on earth is the Holy Spirit. He is taken out of the way at the Rapture and evil is given a free reign. Man, is now left to his own lusts and desires. Evil men will become worse and worse. Man's inhumanity to man will be like no other time in history. Jesus stated clearly that the cataclysms of the Tribulation would be extinction level events. If He does not shorten those days, no flesh would be saved. Life on earth would cease to exist. But He has shortened this period to just seven years.

*"For then shall be **great tribulation**, such as was not since the beginning of the world to this time, no, nor ever shall be. And except those days should be shortened, there should **no flesh be saved**: but for the elect's sake those days shall be shortened."* Matthew 24:21-22

5.3   - Multi-faceted Judgment

The judgments of God that come upon the earth during this time will increase in intensity and frequency. I am talking about massive storms, earthquakes, volcanic eruptions, tsunamis, strange weather patterns, war, famine, disease and death. There will also be strange signs in the sun, moon and stars. Keep an eye out for Planet X or as Gill Broussard calls it, Planet 7X. Check out his work, it is very enlightening.

"And there shall be signs in the sun, and in the moon, and in the stars; and upon the earth distress of nations, with perplexity; the sea and the waves roaring;" Luke 21:25

Many so-called Bible scholars have denied teachings like the Rapture and the seven-year Tribulation. That's a moot point now because, like it or not, you and they are in it.

"Knowing this first, that there shall come in the last days **scoffers**, *walking after their own lusts, And saying, Where is the promise of his coming? for since the fathers fell asleep, all things continue as [they were] from the beginning of the creation." 2 Peter 3:3-4*

5.4   - Purpose of Judgment

The purpose of the increasingly severe judgments of the Tribulation period is threefold;

1. to judge a Christ rejecting world
2. to push Israel to the brink of annihilation so they will finally turn to their Messiah Jesus bringing about the redemption of Israel
3. to drive men to repentance from sin

5.5 - Your Survival

Even though you have given your life to Jesus Christ, you are still here and you will need to survive this Tribulation period.

You probably should start storing at least a 6 months' supply of food and water. Get an alternative to electricity for cooking as there might be extended periods of electrical outages. If you live in a big city you might also consider moving to a rural area. Just don't panic; the Tribulation is seven years long so you have some time to prepare but don't wait too long; start preparing today.

Try to locate a small group of new Christians like yourself. They will prove invaluable when things get tough. I know I am painting a bleak picture but keep the faith and prepare for the worst. You are now a child of the Most High God which will afford you some protection during this time of trouble. God has a way of taking care of His own. But the fact remains that you did not believe while you had the opportunity.

If you survive the seven years you will enter the kingdom of the Lord Jesus Christ that He sets up upon His return. You will enter His kingdom as a mortal human. Your years of healthy life will be greatly extended. If you are martyred during the Tribulation for your faith in Christ, then you will be raised in the resurrection at the second coming of Jesus Christ. Either way you will enter the Kingdom of God, the thousand-year reign of Jesus Christ. I will explain more on this later.

6 Antichrist

6.1 - Rise to Power

The Antichrist comes to prominence on the world scene by confirming the afore mentioned seven-year peace treaty with Israel and several other Middle Eastern nations. As stated, this begins the countdown of the seven-year Tribulation. Seven years from the confirming of the treaty, the entire world will see the coming of the Lord Jesus Christ! If this historic treaty has not been signed, then keep watching the Middle East for it will happen very soon.

This could be an existing treaty like the Oslo Accords or something new. Since this treaty allows the Jews to rebuild the Temple, inaugurate the

27

priesthood and commence animal sacrifices; it could come on the heels of an Israeli victory over some of her nearby belligerent neighbors. Either way, when some agreement is reached with Israel that allows for the Temple and related activities to commence, then the signing of that document starts the seven-year countdown to the second coming of Jesus Christ.

As the new peacemaker in the Middle East, the Antichrist will rise to power within a 10-nation Islamic Confederacy. This Confederacy is the newly revived Islamic Caliphate. The Caliphate will most likely be centered in Turkey, as that was the seat of the old Ottoman Empire. You must keep your eyes on the Middle East, especially Jerusalem; this is where everything will emanate from. Jerusalem is the focal point of the Tribulation events.

6.2 - Weapon of Peace

The Antichrist is a clever master of flattery and deceit. He is a very commanding charismatic speaker mesmerizing his audiences much like Adolf Hitler's hypnotic control over the Germans. These traits accelerate his rise to power as people during the Tribulation are easy prey; looking for any answer to the world's problems. The much-needed Middle East peace plan will garner him tremendous favor and standing with world leaders. But, whatever peace program he implements is just a ruse for him to gain more power. Don't be fooled by all the great press this man receives, he is from the pit of hell. Peace to him is only a weapon of war to conquer the naive and ignorant.

> *"And through his policy also he shall cause craft (deceit and treachery) to prosper in his hand; and he shall magnify [himself] in his heart, and **by peace shall destroy many**: he shall also stand up against the Prince of princes; but he shall be broken without hand." Daniel 8:25 Parenthesis mine*

6.3   - The False Prophet

He is not wearing a name tag reading "Hello, I am the Antichrist", so be aware of his tactics. His modus operandi is peace, flattery, deception, false miracles, lying signs and wonders; especially during the first half of the seven-year Tribulation. The Antichrist has an assistant the Bible calls the "false prophet". He will assist the Antichrist by performing these counterfeit miracles even calling fire down from heaven imitating the prophet Elijah. We will discuss the prophet Elijah in a latter chapter.   Those dazzling signs and wonders are meant to deceive the people into believing the Antichrist is the savior of the world. The False Prophet will be a prominent religious leader seeking to unite the world's religions to worship the Antichrist.

6.4   - Mid-East Caliphate

As the Antichrist rises to control the 10 nation Islamic Coalition, he will become increasingly violent and narcissistic. If you are somewhat familiar with Bible prophecy, the Antichrist is the "little horn" of Daniel chapters 7 and 8 that arises from the region of the ancient Assyrian Empire (Turkey, Syria, Iraq, Lebanon and Jordan.) He is also discussed in Daniel chapter 11.

Note that the Antichrist will introduce economic reforms that will cause nations to prosper. But he is a vain man full of himself and uses peace to deceive and destroy. How does he destroy with peace? By making a peace treaty then breaking the treaty with a surprise attack after the other party feels safe and secure.

*"For yourselves know perfectly that the day of the Lord so cometh as a thief in the night. **For when they shall say, Peace and safety; then sudden destruction cometh upon them**, as travail upon a woman with child; and **they shall not escape**." - 1 Thessalonians 5:2-3*

He is so arrogant that he stands up against Jesus but is quickly destroyed at the second coming of the Lord. More than likely during the first 3 ½ years of the Tribulation he will be Time magazine's Man of the Year. He is a very clever and crafty man that misleads many. His plan is world domination and his program is deception and lies. For the last 3 ½ years he rules the Caliphate. Don't be fooled, keep the faith.

6.5   - Alien Savior

There is another aspect to the Antichrist I want to make you aware of. He might come on the world scene as someone like Adolph Hitler on steroids; a very charismatic leader that solves problems and get things done initially but turns evil. He could also arrive via a fake alien disclosure. A popular theme for the creation of life on earth is that a super-intelligent race of aliens came to earth and seeded life as we know it. Since we are making a mess of the earth, they have come back to put us on the right track and prepare us for the next step in our evolution. The Antichrist could pose as a super-intelligent alien savior come to save mankind and the world.

Yet another idea is that the Antichrist is a physical manifestation of Satan himself. Coming in the form of a man, he unleashes the powers of darkness across the planet. This oppressive cloud of evil could unleash things only seen on television and Si-Fi movies; a real zombie apocalypse; fallen angels, super hybrid humans, warlocks, walking dead, etc. all having a ravenous taste for blood.

Bizarre! Absolutely, but I want you to be aware of some possible scenarios. Whatever form he takes, the Antichrist is empowered by Satan and the powers of darkness. It is by Satan's power that he performs the deceiving lying wonders and fake miracles. Remember, this will be the most horrific period ever to come to planet earth. It is not just another hurricane, earthquake or war; it is global destruction!

6.6   - Extinction Level Events

Jesus said that "**And except those days should be shortened, there should no flesh be saved**: but for the elect's sake those days shall be shortened. Mat 24:22 KJV. That's how bad this seven years will be; mankind would go extinct if Jesus does not return and put a stop to the destruction.

*"Howl ye; for the day of the LORD [is] at hand; **it shall come as a destruction from the Almighty**. ... Behold, the day of the LORD cometh, cruel both with wrath and fierce anger, to lay the land desolate: and he shall destroy the sinners thereof out of it." [Isa 13:6, 9 KJV]*

*"Alas for the day! for the day of the LORD [is] at hand, and as a **destruction from the Almighty** shall it come." [Joe 1:15 KJV]*

*"That day [is] a day of wrath, a day of **trouble** and **distress**, a day of wasteness and **desolation**, a day of darkness and gloominess, a day of clouds and **thick darkness**," [Zep 1:15 KJV]*

Remember, even though all hell seems to be breaking loose, God is in complete control as we will soon see.

7   Antichrist/al-Mahdi

7.1   - The Caliph

The Biblical Antichrist rules a 10-nation Islamic Caliphate in the Middle East. The Muslims refer to the leader of the Caliphate as the "Caliph". The Caliph is the top religious, political, social and military leader of the nations comprising the Caliphate. One might compare the Islamic Caliph and Caliphate for Muslims to the Pope and Vatican for Catholics back in the Middle Ages. Many Bible prophecy scholars, self-included, believe this 10-nation Caliphate will be a revived Ottoman Empire centered in Turkey, hence the Turkish flag above.

Muslim scholars refer to the Caliph of the end times as al-Mahdi. The term means the

"Expected One", the "Hidden One" or the "Promised One." He is the last successor of the prophet Muhammad.

He also has another title, which is the "12th Imam". Muhammad ibn al-Hassan al-Mahdi disappeared into a cave around A.D. 878. He was the 12th Imam from Muhammad and will return in the last days. He is the long awaited "savior" to the Muslims. That is why he has such a tremendous following in the Middle East; a billion Muslims are awaiting his return. But, do not be deceived, He is the Antichrist. Deception, false miracles and lying wonders are his forte. Of course, much of the world will blindly follow him, damning their souls to hell. No matter what he says, do not believe him, he is a liar and a deceiver. I cannot stress this enough as he will be convincing beyond anyone's imagination.

7.2 - Out from the Pit he Arose

Just as the Muslim Mahdi, the 12th Imam, will allegedly come up from a cave or well, the Biblical antichrist will arise from the bottomless pit – hell. Gee, what a coincidence. ☺

"The beast that thou saw... ***shall ascend out of the bottomless pit,*** *and go into perdition (hell): and they that dwell on the earth shall wonder, whose names were not written in the book of life from the foundation of the world, when they behold the beast..."* *Revelation 17:8 (emphasis mine)*

36

7.3   - Two Names Same Guy

Whatever title this Middle East hero uses, he is the Antichrist. The Caliph, the 12th Imam, the Mahdi are all the same person, the Antichrist. Oh yes, in case you are still wondering, he is a Muslim. One might object thinking that the Jews would never accept a Muslim. Well, remember in 1993 when Yitzhak Rabin shook hands confirming the Oslo Accords with Yasser Arafat on the White House lawn with then President Bill Clinton? I rest my case.

Below is a short list of characteristics shared by the Biblical Antichrist and the Muslim al-Mahdi showing that they are one and the same person.

- Both deny the Holy Trinity (Father, Son and Holy Spirit)
- Both deny Jesus' atoning death on the Cross
- Both blaspheme the God of the Bible
- Both are called "the Deceiver" (one of Allah's names is Khayrul-Makireen which means the greatest of all deceivers
- Both work false miracles and lying wonders
- Both ride a white horse
- Both rule over a 10-nation kingdom
- Both bring war and death
- Both arrive with a 7-year peace treaty
- Both destroy by peace

- Both lead a Turkish-Iranian invasion of Israel
- Both desire Israel's destruction
- Both desire world dominance and worship

The above details regarding the Antichrist are from the Holy Bible and the details of al-Mahdi are from Islamic scholars writing about the end times and the Mahdi.

7.4 - Fake Jesus

Muslims have their version of the second coming of Jesus Christ. According to Muslim scholars, Jesus returns as a Muslim and helps the Mahdi convert the world to Islam. He supposedly forces all Christians to convert to Islam or suffer beheading. If someone called "Jesus" (Isa in Islam) appears on the scene prior to the end of the seven-year Tribulation, he is a false Jesus. Do not follow or believe this phony "Jesus". There will be many false messiahs claiming to be Jesus. When the real Jesus Christ returns, there will be no doubt in anyone's mind exactly who He is and what is happening. He is King of Kings, Lord of Lords; full of glory, power and might.

8   The Temple

8.1   - Coming Attractions

As part of the Middle East treaty, the Jews will rebuild their Temple in Jerusalem. We know this must happen because the Antichrist will enter the Temple in the middle of the seven-year Tribulation declaring that he is god. He will set up an image of his kingdom in the Temple and demand all worship it. He will also stop the daily sacrifice performed in the Temple by the Jewish Priests. This act by the Antichrist defiles the Temple of God and is called by the prophet Daniel and the Lord Jesus, the "Abomination of Desolation." It is an abomination that defiles the

Temple and makes it desolate of the presence of God.

*"Who opposeth and exalteth himself above all that is called God, or that is worshipped; so that **he as God sitteth in the temple of God, shewing himself that he is God**." 2Thessalonians 2:4*

8.2 - Let's Build It

For several years, the Jewish rabbis have been preparing to rebuild the Temple. The Temple Institute was formed to prepare the priestly garments and temple vessels of sacrifice and worship. They have also been training priests for Temple worship and sacrifices. As of this writing, everything is ready and waiting on the structure to be built. The Sanhedrin have even appointed a High Priest to preside over temple activities. Perhaps, as you read, construction has already started or even been completed.

8.3 - Antichrist Want's the Temple

The Antichrist will be a proponent of rebuilding the Temple because he knows that the Temple in Jerusalem is the true earthly Temple of the Living God and not the Kaaba, or the Black Stone, in Mecca. In the middle of the Tribulation he makes his move to take control of the Temple and demands people worship him. The open area to the right of the Dome of the Rock is where the Tribulation Temple could be built. There is also talk of building the Jewish Temple where the Al-Aqsa mosque now stands. If it is not under construction, it soon will be.

The Antichrist desires to rule his kingdom from Jerusalem and beat Jesus to the punch, so to speak. He, the Antichrist, wants to rule and reign over this earth for a thousand years. When Jesus returns at the end of the Tribulation, He will rule the earth with a rod of iron from Jerusalem. The Antichrist is trying to get there first and lay his claim to the throne. He is a pretender to the throne and Jesus will deal with him speedily upon His second coming.

The Antichrist and Islam are the antithesis of Jesus and the Bible. Whatever God is doing with respect to Bible prophecy, Satan and the Antichrist are either trying to destroy, corrupt or subvert it. With respect to the Temple in Jerusalem, scripture tells us that Jesus will rule and reign from there while His Millennial Temple is being built (Ezekiel Ch. 40-48). The Antichrist, however, wants to get there first and set up his earthly kingdom. As with all the devil's plans, the Antichrist's reign from Jerusalem is short lived ending in his destruction.

9 Abomination of Desolation

9.1 - An Evil Coronation

I have previously mentioned the "Abomination of Desolation" but let's take a closer look. More than likely this event will be on main stream media for all to see, so you need to know what's happening. At the middle of the seven-year Tribulation the Antichrist will enter the Temple in Jerusalem and set up an image of his kingdom. He will then proclaim himself to be god.

Much pomp and fanfare will surround this occasion as he is trying to usurp Almighty God. It will be quite a spectacle. Extravagant Olympic opening ceremonies, stately Presidential inaugurations and even lavish Royal Weddings will pale in comparison to the magnificent grandeur of this event. The leader of the New World Order is taking his rightful place on the throne; or so they think. Almighty God has a different opinion.

Erecting an image to the Antichrist's kingdom in the Temple is the abomination. This image is a false idol, a detestable abomination to the Lord Jesus Christ. The desolation aspect of the phrase means the presence of the Lord has departed the Holy Temple because of the abomination. So, the phrase "Abomination of Desolation" refers to a pagan idol set up in the Temple at Jerusalem that makes the Temple desolate of God's presence.

9.2 - Worship Me of Die

The Antichrist and his right-hand man, the false prophet, will demand all to worship him or else suffer death. He will make fire come down from heaven and do other lying miracles and false wonders to deceive people. This is big screen Hollywood special effects entertainment in real time. The Antichrist will seem almost indestructible, as many will worship him. Everyone that does not bow and worship him will have a death sentence on their head.

"And they worshipped the dragon which gave power unto the beast (Antichrist): and they worshipped

44

the beast, saying, Who [is] like unto the beast? who is able to make war with him?" - Revelation 13:4 parenthesis mine

9.3   - The Terrible Twosome

These details are found in Revelation chapter 13 where the Apostle John describes two beasts. The first beast (v.1-10) is the 10-nation kingdom of the Antichrist, a revived Islamic Caliphate over which he rules for 3 ½ years. The term "beast" refers to both the Antichrist and his kingdom. The second beast is the false prophet (v. 11-18) that performs great deceiving wonders and causes all that do not worship the first beast to be killed. Remember, they are both deceivers. They perform false miracles and lying wonders to deceive many and sadly, many will follow them.

*"And for this cause God shall send them strong delusion, that **they should believe a lie**: That they all might be damned who **believed not the truth**, but had pleasure in unrighteousness." - 2 Thessalonians 2:11-12*

9.4   - Deception, Deception, Deception

The lying signs and wonders they perform are very real and key to their deception. These false miracles are accepted by many as proof that the Antichrist and false prophet are the real deal. Even though their powers are great and their miracles real they are not from Almighty God. That is why they are called "lying" signs and wonders, because they are from the powers of hell. The Antichrist and false prophet want to deceive as many people as possible so they can take their souls to hell.

During Jesus' ministry, He did many miracles. But those miracles were for the glory of the Father and to validate Jesus ministry and who He claimed to be, the Son of God. When the false prophet does his lying miracles, they are for the purpose of deception. To con people into believing that he and the Antichrist are something they are not.

Keep your faith and testimony in the Lord Jesus Christ and never depart from it. You know the truth so do not believe anything the Antichrist or false prophet say or do. They are liars and desire to condemn your soul to hell for an eternal swim in the lake of fire.

"And then shall that Wicked (Antichrist) be revealed, whom the Lord shall consume with the spirit of his mouth, and shall destroy with the brightness of his coming: [Even him], **whose coming is after the working of Satan with all power and signs and lying wonders***, And with all deceivableness of unrighteousness in them that perish; because they received not the love of the truth, that they might be saved." 2Thessalonians 2:8-10 Parenthesis mine*

"And he does **great wonders***, so that* **he makes fire come down from heaven** *on the earth*

in the sight of men, And **deceives them that dwell on the earth by [the means of] those miracles** *which he had power to do in the sight of the beast; saying to them that dwell on the earth, that they should make an image to the beast, which had the wound by a sword, and did live." Revelation 13:13-14*

10   Birth Pangs

10.1 - A Process of Death

The increasingly catastrophic events of the Tribulation are frequently referred to in the Bible as "sorrows" and equated to a woman having "birth pangs." The idea is that birth pangs grow more intense and occur more frequently as delivery approaches. **Things will get increasingly worse as the second coming of Jesus Christ approaches**. Associated with the beginning birth pangs are wars, famines, pestilence and earthquakes.

Wars are fairly obvious as they receive considerable news coverage. However, famines are more subtle, inflicting a slow death upon populations generally in poorer countries. The

Russian famine of 1921 starved over 5 million people. The Soviet Union Ukraine famine of 1932 killed 7-10 million people. The great Chinese famine of 1959 killed upwards of 40 million people. The Congo famine of 1998 took the lives of almost 4 million people. Famines take years to play out and are not as dramatic as warfare but just as deadly.

Pestilence and disease also kill millions in a subtle way as people just get sick and die. The threat of a pandemic is seemingly always with us. Bird flu, swine flu, HIV aids and Ebola are some of the current threats to human health. Each year malaria kills over 3 million people. Twenty million die each year from Schistosomiasis. Tuberculosis and typhoid each kill around 2 million people each year as of 2015. Sadly, the death tolls from famine and disease during the Tribulation will be beyond pandemic.

10.2 - Bad to Worse

As you move further into the Tribulation period, wars, famine, disease and earthquakes will increase in frequency and intensity. The destruction of war brings famine and famine brings disease. The earthquakes and disease will kill many people. There will also be an increase in other natural disasters like storms, volcanic eruptions, mass animal deaths, meteors hitting the earth and strange activity in the sun, moon and stars. At least half the population of planet earth will die during the seven-year tribulation, most in the second half. As I write this almost 4 billion people will die from these events.

The pattern should be clear: war, famine, disease, earthquakes and death. As these events unfold, many people will panic because they don't know the truth of what is happening. Chaos, burning, looting, anarchy, death and destruction will be on a scale previously unheard of. But you now know the truth, so don't panic, all this must happen before the Lord returns. Hang in there and do not give up your faith in Jesus. Always remember, The Lord Jesus Christ is running the entire program from the throne room of heaven. It may look like the Devil is in charge but he isn't.

10.3 - The Four Horsemen Ride

Birth pangs of war, famine and disease are taught in Matthew Ch. 24 as discussed in the next chapter. They are also taught in the book of Revelation Ch. 6 as the Lord breaks the seven seals on the scroll the title deed to the earth. The first four seals are commonly named the Four Horseman of the Apocalypse. Let's look at the Four Horsemen from the Book of Revelation Ch. 6. The Apostle John has been caught up to the throne of God in heaven and told to write down in a book everything he sees.

*"And I saw when the Lamb(Jesus) opened one of the seals, and I heard, as it were the noise of thunder, one of the four beasts(living creatures) saying, Come and see. And I saw, and behold a **white horse**: and he that sat on him had a **bow**; and a **crown** was given unto him: and he went forth conquering, and to **conquer.**" Revelation 6:1-2*

10.4 - White Horse – Fake Savior

As the first seal is broken, a white horse and rider come forth. The rider is given a crown and a bow, symbolic of power and military might. This rider is a false messiah coming on a white horse imitating the Lord Jesus Christ. He is the Antichrist, and is sent forth to conquer nations. He does this by deceitful peace. The prophet Daniel said it best:

*"And his power shall be mighty, but not by his own power (he is empowered by Satan): and he shall destroy wonderfully, and shall prosper, and practice (his own will), and shall destroy the mighty and the holy people (the Jews and Christians). And through his policy also he shall cause craft (deceit and treachery) to prosper in his hand; and he shall magnify [himself] in his heart, **and by peace shall destroy many**: he shall also stand up against the Prince of princes (Jesus Christ); but he shall be broken without hand." Dan 8:24-25 Parentheses Mine*

How does the Antichrist destroy using peace? This is an old Muslim tactic first used by Muhammad back in the 7th century and still part of their global strategy. In 628 A. D. Muhammad, while living in Medina, signed a treaty with the people of Mecca.

The Treaty of Hudaibiya was for 10 years of peace. After 2 years Muhammad attacked Mecca by surprise and defeated them. This tactic has been called a Hudna down through the ages. You make a peace treaty with your enemy to buy time to build up your armies and weapons for a surprise attack. This is how the Antichrist will begin his campaign of conquest; false peace and deception. As King Solomon wisely said, "There is nothing new under the sun."

It's interesting that Muslim scholars writing on the end times proclaim that their Mahdi is the rider of the white horse.

10.5 - War and Famine

"And there went out another **horse [that was] red**: and [power] was given to him that sat thereon to **take peace from the earth**, and that they should kill one another: and there was given unto him a **great sword**." Revelation 6:4

The second seal brings the red horse of war. The rider is given power to take peace from the earth and a great sword is given to him. The red horse rider follows the Antichrist's false peace. War

53

is ever present during the seven-year Tribulation. The third seal releases a black horse. The rider has a pair of scales in his hand to measure food. This is symbolic of food shortages for the common people resulting in famine. However, the rich fare much better as the "oil and wine" are protected.

*"And when he had opened the third seal, I heard the third beast say, Come and see. And I beheld, and lo a **black horse**; and he that sat on him had a **pair of balances** in his hand. And I heard a voice in the midst of the four beasts say, A measure of wheat for a penny, and three measures of barley for a penny; and [see] thou hurt not the oil and the wine." Revelation 6:5-6*

10.6 - Pale Rider - Death

The fourth seal is very ominous as a pale green horse comes forth whose rider is Death, and Hell follows close behind him. From the actions and destruction perpetrated on the people of earth by the first three horsemen, many will die and be cast into hell. One fourth of the population of planet earth will die from the Four Horsemen.

*"And when he had opened **the fourth seal**, I heard the voice of the fourth beast say, Come and see. And I looked, and behold a **pale horse**: and his name that sat on him was **Death, and Hell followed with him**. And power was given unto them over **the fourth part of the earth**, to kill with **sword**, and with*

*hunger, and with **death**, and with the **beasts of the earth**." Revelation 6:7-8*

The phrase "beasts of the earth" is an interesting phrase as it does not simply refer to wild animals. The phrase speaks of bestial men set on the destruction of humanity. These are either demonically possessed people or manifestations of demons and fallen angels; possibly like the Walking Dead on steroids. With recent strides in genetic research the possibility of genetically enhanced humans is becoming a reality. Trans-humanism is a very popular topic these days as scientists manipulate human DNA, combining it with animal DNA. Who knows what these neo-Frankensteinian mad scientists will try to develop?

10.7 - Martyrs for Christ

The fifth seal testifies to the souls of martyrs for Christ that are now in heaven with the Lord. These are they which believed in Jesus during the seven-year Tribulation and were martyred for their faith. Their soul and spirit are with the Lord and their bodies will be resurrected at the second coming of Jesus Christ at the end of the seven-year Tribulation.

The sixth seal calls for a great earthquake that darkens the skies. A horrific meteor shower pummels the earth. Mountains are toppled and islands fall into the sea. People try to hide in caves and underground bunkers but to no avail. There is no place to hide from the wrath of God.

As you can clearly see things are going from bad to worse as the seven-year Tribulation progresses. If you are in the middle of all this, be strong in your faith in Jesus Christ. Your reward in heaven will be great. Don't yield to those that would have you follow the Antichrist. Stand strong in the face of fear and calamity as all these horrific events are under Jesus Christ's direct control and His purpose is being worked out; to destroy the Antichrist, his kingdom and followers.

10.8 - The Ottoman Seal

Above is the seal and symbol of the Ottoman Empire. There are several interesting features of this seal that follow the first three Horsemen of the Apocalypse. In the first horseman, the Antichrist, is given a bow and sent forth to conquer. In the bottom center of the seal below the oval is a bow and two quivers of arrows. The stylized script at the top center translates to "may the Caliph be

57

victorious". In the actual symbol the name of the Caliph would be used.

The second horseman is that of war. He is given a great sword symbolizing great and powerful weapons of mass destruction. If you look at the seal there are many weapons on the seal; spears, swords and even a handgun.

The third horseman is the black horse of famine. Many people will die from famine during the Tribulation. Interesting that on the Ottoman seal there is scale or balance on the left of the image. During the Tribulation, food will be sold in small quantities by weight. I am sure if you asked a Muslim familiar with the Ottoman Empire their symbols would have a different meaning but they are there in the seal nonetheless and in the Apostle John's writings in the Book of Revelation

The center of the Ottoman Empire was Turkey. In the 20th century Turkey was a cosmopolitan nation seeking to be a bridge between Europe and the Middle East. They were even seeking to join the European Union. Then the Islamist APK party took political power and everything began to change and change quickly. A onetime ally of Israel, Turkey quickly became an enemy.

Just today as I am writing, I read an article stating that the Turkish Prime Minister joined by the leader of Hamas were praising the coming war with Israel wherein Turkey would liberate

58

Jerusalem and the Al-Aqsa mosque. Here is a direct quote from the article: "As Turkey for centuries was the main defender of Jerusalem and Al-Aqsa Mosque, likewise with you are the center of the Muslim Ummah (Muslim nation) which will carry on the mission of liberating Jerusalem and al-Aqsa Mosque."

This is a direct reference to the Ottoman Empire as the defender of Jerusalem and the Al-Aqsa mosque. The Ottoman Empire is rising again. Perhaps as you read this, it is already risen from the desert sands and wielding much power.

11 A Private Briefing

11.1 - 2nd Temple Destruction

In the Book of Matthew chapters 24 and 25 Jesus gives what is referred to as the Olivet Discourse, a private briefing to His disciples about the last day's events just prior to His second coming. I want to give this some attention as it is an integral part of end time prophecy. Grab your King James Bible and follow along.

Jesus says to the disciples in chapter 24 verse 2 pertaining to the Temple *"There shall not be left here one stone upon another, that shall not be thrown down."* The destruction of the Jewish Temple occurred in 70 A.D. perpetrated by the Roman legions under the command of General Titus. But Jesus did not return in 70 A.D. so the remainder of the prophecy is yet future as of this writing.

11.2 - Deception – Multiple Warnings

Jesus' statement about the destruction of the Temple prompts the disciples question in verse 3 *"Tell us, when shall these things be? and what [shall be] the sign of thy coming, and of the end of the world?"* Jesus first statement to His disciples was *"Take heed that no man deceive you. For many shall come in my name, saying, I am Christ; and shall deceive many."* Deception by a false Christ (Antichrist) will be rampant during the seven-year Tribulation. Deception will be the hallmark of Antichrist's rule and many will fall for his lies, don't be one of them.

11.3 - Birth Pangs Begin

Jesus continues with *"And ye shall hear of **wars and rumors of wars**: see that ye be not troubled: for all [these things] must come to pass, but the end is not yet. For nation shall rise against nation, and kingdom against kingdom: and there shall be **famines, and pestilences, and earthquakes, in diverse places**. All these [are] the beginning of sorrows."* Wars and rumors of wars exist now and will continue into the Tribulation. It seems like there is always some nation rattling their sword threatening war. The birth pangs begin with a convergence of end time

Pocket Guide to the Tribulation

signs and everything will increase in intensity from there.

Wars are generally followed by famine and pestilences. By these many people will die from massive food shortages and diseases that naturally follow periods of famine. Malnutrition breeds disease. Earthquakes will also take many lives as we have already witnessed in the Japan tsunami killing 280,000 or the great China earthquake of 1976 killing 600,000. We just read the parallel to this in the previous chapter with the Four Horsemen of the Apocalypse from the Book of Revelation chapter 6.

11.4 - Tribulation Martyrs

In Matthew Ch. 24 verse 9 Jesus declares *"Then shall they deliver you up to be afflicted, and **shall kill you**: and ye shall be hated of all nations for my name's sake."* Many professing faith in Jesus Christ during the Tribulation will be beaten, tortured and killed for their testimony of faith in Jesus. They will refuse to take the mark of the beast. They will stand for Jesus Christ and not become slaves to the Antichrist's new global system. It will cost many their lives.

"And then shall many be offended, and shall betray one another, and shall hate one another." Many that claim to be Christians will be offended, that is, they will stumble and fall from the faith because they are not willing to give their life for their testimony. They will betray true Christians

to gain favor with the authorities. People will do just about anything to ensure their survival. These false believers will turn on Christians and hate them. Watch out for such people as they will betray you. Be very careful of who you befriend in these last days.

11.5 - Fake Prophets

Jesus continues in verse 11 with *"And **many false prophets shall rise, and shall deceive many**. And because iniquity shall abound, the love of many shall wax cold. But he that shall endure unto the end, the same shall be saved."* Here again Jesus warns believers of mass deception. Many will be deceived because they do not know or love the truth of the Bible. Sin will abound and godly love will all but vanish. Jesus commands those that love Him to "endure unto the end." If you endure to the end of the Tribulation, until His second coming, you will be saved. That is, you will enter the Kingdom of God and be spared the fires of hell.

11.6 - An Old Gospel

Jesus then states *"And this **gospel of the kingdom** shall be preached in all the world for a witness unto all nations; and then shall the end come."* This is a point that few understand. During the Tribulation, the gospel of the kingdom is preached, not the gospel of grace that was preached before the Rapture. The gospel of the kingdom is "repent for the kingdom of God is at hand." This gospel was preached by John the Baptist and Jesus during the early days of Jesus' ministry. Jesus stopped preaching the gospel of the kingdom once He was officially rejected by the Jews in Matthew Ch. 12. From then on Jesus taught in parables because the kingdom was no longer at hand. Since Jesus is returning in a few short years, the kingdom of God is again at hand. Hold tight to your profession of faith in Jesus until the end and you will enter the kingdom.

11.7 - The Midpoint

"*When ye therefore shall see the* **abomination of desolation**, *spoken of by Daniel the prophet, stand in the holy place, (whoso readeth, let him understand).*" At this point in the Olivet Discourse we are at the midpoint of the seven-year Tribulation. Here Jesus makes a reference to the Abomination of Desolation spoken of by the prophet Daniel. The Antichrist will perpetrate this event by placing an image of his kingdom in the newly rebuilt Temple in Jerusalem and proclaim himself god.

"*Who opposeth and exalteth himself above all that is called God, or that is worshipped;* **so that he as God sitteth in the temple of God, shewing himself that he is God**." - *2 Thessalonians 2:4 KJV*

Jesus tells those that live in and around Jerusalem to flee into the mountains and hide out for the last half of the Tribulation period.

In verse 22 Jesus begins the second half of the Tribulation by stating *"For then shall be **great tribulation**, such as was not since the beginning of the world to this time, no, nor ever shall be. And except those days should be shortened, there should no flesh be saved: but for the elect's sake those days shall be shortened."*

Jesus proclaims the second half of the Tribulation will be the most horrific 3 ½ years the earth has ever experienced. If this period were to continue longer that 3 ½ years, then no one would be saved. You must endure this period of catastrophic events so get prepared and keep the faith.

11.8 - More Deception

Again, in verse 24 Jesus warns of false Christ's with *"For there shall arise **false Christs, and false prophets,** and shall shew great signs and wonders; insomuch that, if [it were] possible, they shall deceive the very elect. Behold, I have told you before."* You must understand that deception will be of epic proportions as Jesus gives more warnings about deception than anything else. Deception is so great and powerful that many will fall to its lure. Only those that love the truth and know the Word of God will recognize the propaganda for what it actually is; pure unadulterated lies from hell designed for one purpose, to promote the lie that the Antichrist is god. The source of these lies is Satan himself and the vehicle for dissemination is the government controlled media.

Jesus continues by making a reference to Mecca; *"Wherefore if they shall say unto you, Behold, he is **in the desert**; go not forth: behold, [he is] in the **secret chambers**; believe [it] not."* The Antichrist will proclaim himself ruler of Islam, the Mahdi, from Mecca which is in the Arabian Desert. Jesus is not coming from the desert or the secret chambers of the Vatican or the Masonic Lodge either.

11.9 - The Return of the King of Kings

The true Christ, Jesus Christ, will return ***"as the lightning cometh out of the east, and shineth even unto the west; so shall also the coming of the Son of man be."*** The return of the Lord Jesus will be the most spectacular event of all history and seen by all. Bright as the sun and as shockingly brilliant as lightening He will part the eastern sky over Jerusalem. He will not need CNN to announce His coming as the entire world will know when He appears.

Jesus then describes the atmospheric conditions on the earth at His coming with "*Immediately after the tribulation of those days shall the **sun be darkened**, and the **moon shall not give her light**, and the stars shall fall from heaven, and the powers of the **heavens shall be shaken**.*" The atmosphere is darkened with smoke, dust and other particles from all the cataclysmic events that have taken place during the Tribulation. The sun and moon are darkened and the stars appear to have all fallen because starlight is not strong enough to penetrate the polluted atmosphere.

"*And then shall appear the sign of the Son of man in heaven: and then shall all the tribes of the earth mourn, and they shall see the **Son of man coming in the clouds of heaven with power and great glory**.*" Jesus will return in the clouds of heaven with power and great glory to defeat His enemies and the enemies of Israel. The Jews will mourn as they realize that their coming Messiah visited them two thousand years ago, and they rejected Him. They will see the one they pierced (on the cross), the one that was wounded in the house of His friends, the Jews.

"*And I will pour upon the house of David, and upon the inhabitants of Jerusalem, the spirit of grace and of supplications: and **they shall look upon me whom they have pierced**, and they shall mourn for* *him, as **one mourns for [his] only [son]**, and shall be in bitterness for him, as one that is in bitterness for [his] firstborn." Zechariah 12:10*

Jesus has returned. The Jews realize exactly who He is and bitterly mourn. They are in great sorrow, lamenting the fact that their ancestors crucified their true King two thousand years ago. After the mourning, Jews from all across the globe are gathered to Jerusalem to celebrate Jesus return and coronate Him as King. *"And he shall send his angels with a great sound of a trumpet, and they shall **gather together his elect from the four winds**, from one end of heaven to the other."*

11.10 - The Last Generation

Jesus now offers the parable of the fig tree stating *"Now learn a parable of the fig tree; When his branch is yet tender, and putteth forth leaves, ye know that summer [is] nigh: So likewise ye, **when ye shall see all these things, know that it is near, [even] at the doors.**"* When the fig tree blooms then you know that summer is near. When you see Christmas decorations in the mall then you know that Thanksgiving is near. ☺

The fig tree is a symbol for the nation of Israel. Israel became a nation state in 1948. Jesus states ***"Verily I say unto you, This generation shall not pass, till all these things be fulfilled."*** The generation that witnessed the rebirth of Israel will not pass before

69

the second coming of the Lord Jesus Christ. The words of Jesus are sure and true, *"Heaven and earth shall pass away, but my words shall not pass away."*

There are several numbers in scripture that relate to a generation. 40 years, 70 years and 120 years are notable. But which number relates to the end times, the days in which we live? 40 does not as 40 years have already passed since 1948. 120 years does not because people do not live that long today. The only candidate is 70 years. The scripture adds another 10 years for healthy people. 70 to 80 years fits perfectly into the end times prophetic window. The second coming of Jesus Christ and the catastrophic events preceding it will be completed by 2028. That includes the seven-year Tribulation. Jesus also said He would shorten those days so it could erupt any moment as I write. You might already be in it as you read.

11.11 - The Days of Noah

Jesus changes gears and relates His second coming to the days of Noah stating "***But as the days of Noah were, so shall also the coming of the Son of man be***. *For as in the days that were before the flood they were eating and drinking, marrying and giving in marriage, until the day that Noe entered into the ark, And* **knew not until the flood came, and took them all**

away*; so shall also the coming of the Son of man be."*

The point is that people in Noah's day paid no attention to him building an arc and preaching about the impending judgment. They just went about their daily lives and ignored Noah's warnings to repent. No one believed him until the day the rains came and the flood waters took them away. But of course, by then it was too late. So, it will be at the second coming of the Lord Jesus Christ. Many will not believe until it is too late, too late to repent and believe.

But there was something else happening back then also. In the days of Noah there were giants on the earth. They were the Nephilim, the offspring of fallen angels mating with human women.

*"There were **giants in the earth in those days***; and also after that, when the sons of God came in unto the daughters of men, and they bare [children] to them, the same [became] mighty men which [were] of old, men of renown." - Genesis 6:4*

There is much evidence in archeology for the existence of giants and many believe they will return during the seven-year Tribulation. These creatures might be viewed as aliens but are actually demonic. If they do return everyone will know it. There might be some very bizarre creatures on the earth so watch and be aware of what they are and their origin. Just recently the Smithsonian Institute was forced to reveal that they have been covering up and destroying giant human remains found in America since the early 1900s.

Some believe that the phrases "eating and drinking" and "marrying and giving in marriage" depict life as usual. If that be the case, then what is so prophetic about that? Nothing, really. So why would Jesus mention it? Well, that is not what is meant. The giants, the Nephilim, had voracious appetites even to the extent of eating humans and each other. The extra-biblical books of Enoch and Jasher talk about the giants drinking the blood of animals and humans. So, the phrase "eating and drinking" refers to giants eating flesh and drinking blood. "Marrying and giving in marriage" refers to giants taking human women for wives and having more Nephilim children. I know this sounds bizarre, but watch for it.

Just as in Noah's flood the unbelievers were taken away by the flood waters, the same situation will occur at the second coming when *"Then shall two be in the field; the **one shall be taken, and the other left**. Two [women shall be] grinding at the mill; the one shall be taken, and the other left. **Watch therefore**: for ye know not what hour your Lord doth come."* Unbelievers will be taken away and cast into the fires of hell (see the wheat and tares parable in the Gospel of Matthew chapter 13). Believers are left and will enter the kingdom.

Also, you do not know the exact day and hour so be prepared always.

11.12 - Be Ready Always

Jesus next relates the timing of His second coming to a homeowner stating *"But know this, that if the goodman of the house had known in what watch the thief would come, he would have watched, and would not have suffered his house to be broken up.* **Therefore be ye also ready**: *for in such an hour as ye think not the Son of man cometh."* The continuing message is watch and always be ready for His return. Let nothing in the world move you from this mindset.

"Who then is a faithful and wise servant, whom his lord hath made ruler over his household, to give them meat in due season? Blessed [is] that servant, whom his lord when he cometh shall find so doing. Verily I say unto you, That he shall make him ruler over all his goods." You be that faithful servant that is walking in your faith and doing the Lords business when He returns.

"But and if that evil servant shall say in his heart, My lord delayeth his coming; And shall begin to smite [his] fellow servants, and to eat and drink with the drunken; The lord of that servant shall come in a day when he looketh not for [him], and in an hour that he is not aware of, And shall cut him asunder, and appoint [him] his portion with the hypocrites: there shall be weeping and

gnashing of teeth." The evil servant goes the way of the world and his lord's return is a surprise. He is rewarded with the fires of hell where there is weeping and gnashing of teeth. Keep the faith and watch. The good servant is rewarded and made ruler over his master's possessions. As true believers in Jesus Christ we will rule and reign with Him in His Kingdom. So, be about the business of the Lord Jesus Christ doing whatever he has for you to do. Seek Him daily for His will for your life.

11.13 - Watch Always

Jesus continues the theme watch and be ready in Matthew chapter 25. He begins with the parable of the 10 virgins, five wise and five foolish. The five wise virgins were prepared for the bridegroom and went into the marriage reception. The five foolish virgins were unprepared for the bridegroom's arrival and did not enter the reception supper. Jesus sums it up with ***"Watch therefore**, for ye know neither the day nor the hour wherein the Son of man cometh."* This cannot be stressed enough. Watch and be ready for the Lord's return. Notice that at first all 10 virgins seemed to be ready and prepared as they all had oil in their lamps. However, only 5 were truly prepared by having extra provisions. The 5 foolish were only spectators not prepared for what was to come.

11.14 - Use Your Time and Resources Wisely

Jesus continues in Matthew chapter 25 with the parable of the talents. *"For [the kingdom of heaven is] as a man travelling into a far country, [who] called his own servants, and delivered unto them his goods. And unto one he gave five talents, to another two, and to another one; to every man according to his several ability; and straightway took his journey."* A man leaves his business in the hands of three servants while he travels to a far country. The servants are to do his business while he is away.

"Then he that had received the five talents went and traded with the same, and made [them] other five talents." The servant with five talents did his masters biding and earned five more for his master. *"And likewise he that [had received] two, he also gained other two."* The servant that received two talents earned an additional two talents for his master. These two servants were obedient to the will of their master just as we Christians are to be obedient to the will of Jesus Christ for our lives and be faithful witnesses for Jesus.

"But he that had received one went and digged in the earth, and hid his lord's money." This servant did not invest the one talent but hid it in the earth. But after a long while the owner returned and wanted an account from his servants. The first

two servants did well and were both rewarded. But the servant with only one talent had a different story.

"Then he which had received the one talent came and said, Lord, I knew thee that thou art an hard man, reaping where thou hast not sown, and gathering where thou hast not strawed: And I was afraid, and went and hid thy talent in the earth: lo, [there] thou hast [that is] thine." The master was very displeased with this servant for not using the talent for the masters business. This is a disobedient servant who did not do the will of his master and therefore suffers greatly in outer darkness. Stand for Jesus and do His will so you do not suffer the same fate. *"Take therefore the talent from him, and give [it] unto him which hath ten talents."* His lone talent was given to the servant with ten talents. The servant who received one talent was cast into outer darkness where there is weeping and gnashing of teeth. Doesn't sound like a place I want to live. Keep the faith.

Next Jesus makes an interesting statement: *"For unto every one that hath shall be given, and he shall have abundance: but from him that hath not shall be taken away even that which he hath."* He that obeys his master and does his business will be rewarded. But he that does not obey even what he has will be taken away and given to the obedient. Keep the faith and do the Lord's will.

When Jesus returns, he will gather the nations and separate them. "***And he shall set the sheep on his right hand, but the goats on the left.*** *Then shall the King say unto them on his right hand, Come, ye blessed of my Father, inherit the kingdom prepared for you from the foundation of the world.*" The righteous sheep will enter the kingdom. This judgment is based on how these nations treated Gods people. Jesus states "*Inasmuch as ye have done [it] unto one of the least of these my brethren, ye have done [it] unto me.*" Those nations that treat God's brethren fairly will enter the kingdom. Those nations that treat God's people badly will be cast into everlasting punishment. "*Inasmuch as ye did [it] not to one of the least of these, ye did [it] not to me. And these shall go away into everlasting punishment: but the righteous into life eternal.*" Keep the faith and be counted among the righteous.

12 Two Witnesses

12.1 - A True Dynamic Duo

Tourism may be down in the Holy Land but two Jewish men will appear in Jerusalem seemingly from out of nowhere. The Bible speaks of them as two olive trees that stand before God. As the above olive trees are from ancient times so are these two witnesses. There is much speculation as to their identity. Some say they are Elijah and Moses, others say they are Elijah and Enoch. The reason Enoch is not one of the two witnesses is the following scripture.

*"By faith Enoch was translated that **he should not see death**; and was not found, because God had*

Pocket Guide to the Tribulation

translated him: for before his translation he had this testimony, that he pleased God." - Hebrews 11:5 KJV

The text clearly states that Enoch would "not see death." That means that Enoch was not translated so he could come back and a later time and die. So, the two witnesses are Moses and Elijah, the same two Jesus met with on the Mount of Transfiguration (Matthew 17:2-3). These two witnesses for the Lord prophecy for 42 months (3 ½ years). They appear after the Temple is rebuilt in Jerusalem. Watch for them as they will be on television regularly. However, they will speak the truth so their media time might be cut short. You know how the media loves the truth ☺.

We know that Elijah is one of the two witnesses. His coming is foretold in the last book of the Old Testament as coming in the days prior to the second coming of Jesus Christ.

*"Behold, **I will send my messenger**, and he shall prepare the way before me: and the Lord, whom ye seek, shall **suddenly come to his temple**, even the messenger of the covenant, whom ye delight in: behold, he shall come, saith the LORD of hosts." Malachi 3:1*

12.2 - Light My Fire

These two witnesses have some very peculiar characteristics such as no one will be able to hurt them until their ministry is complete. If someone tries they will be consumed by fire.

*"And I will give [power] unto **my two witnesses**, and they shall prophesy a thousand two hundred [and] threescore days, clothed in sackcloth. ... And if any man will hurt them, **fire proceedeth out of their mouth, and devoureth their enemies**: and if any man will hurt them, he must in this manner be killed." Revelation 11:3, 5*

12.3 - Rain, Rain Go Away

They will stop rain for 42 months. They turn water into blood and cause plagues to come upon the earth. The purpose of these plagues and judgments is to force people to repent of their sins. The sad fact is that most do not repent but become increasingly hostile in their hatred and rebellion against the Lord Jesus Christ.

*"These have power to **shut heaven, that it rain not** in the days of their prophecy: and have power over waters to **turn them to blood**, and to **smite the earth with all plagues**, as often as they will." Revelation 11:6*

12.4 - They're Alive

After they have finished their testimony they will be killed by the Antichrist. Their dead bodies will lie in the street in Jerusalem for three days. The Antichrist and his crowd will celebrate their death by having parties and exchanging gifts. But after the three days they will come back to life, stand to their feet and ascend up to heaven while their enemies are watching. Of course, the main stream media will be dumb founded as they offer up lame explanations for this event; perhaps another alien abduction.

> *"And when they shall have finished their testimony, the beast... shall make war against them, and shall overcome them, and* **kill them**. *And their dead bodies [shall lie] in the street of Jerusalem. And they of the people and kindreds and tongues and nations shall see their dead bodies three days and an half, and shall not suffer their dead bodies to be put in graves. And they that dwell upon the* **earth shall rejoice over them, and make merry, and shall send gifts one to another;** *because these two prophets tormented them that dwelt on the earth. And after three days and an half the Spirit of life from God entered into them, and* **they stood upon their feet;** *and great fear fell upon them which saw them. And they heard a great voice from heaven saying unto them, Come up hither. And* **they ascended up to heaven in a cloud; and their enemies beheld them.**" *Revelation 11:7-12*

I know, it sounds rather bizarre. But remember, you are in the most unusual and horrific period in the history of the planet. Pay close attention to the testimony of these two Prophets of

God and do whatever they say. Their message will be repentance from sin and coming judgments.

12.5 - 144,000 Preachers

Also around the time of the appearing of the Two Witnesses after the building of the Temple in Jerusalem, 144,000 men are sealed from the 12 tribes of ancient Israel for service to God. Who they are and how this will happen only God knows. But I believe they will be evangelists going throughout the world bearing witness to the Lord Jesus Christ.

And I heard the number of them which were sealed: [and there were] sealed an hundred [and] forty [and] four thousand of all the tribes of the children of Israel. - Revelation 7:4 KJV

13 The Mark of the Beast

13.1 - What is the Mark?

No, the mark of the beast is not an ear tag found on most livestock. But it seems like everyone has an opinion on what it might be. People thought it was the social security number, the plastic credit card or the credit card with an embedded chip. Who can forget the ranting when the barcode became a universal branding? And finally, the most recent craze, the RFID chip implanted under the skin.

Although the RFID chip implant makes perfect sense for Western and non-Muslim nations, can you imagine hundreds of millions of Muslims in the Middle East willingly accepting a western technology electronic device implanted under their skin? No way, that is not going to happen. But it does not need happen to fulfill the prophetic scriptures.

"And that no man might buy or sell, save he that had the mark, or the name of the beast, or the number of his name." - Revelation 13:17 KJV

Notice there are three methods of being approved to buy and sell.
1. Having the Mark
2. Having the Name
3. Having the Number of the Name

If you have one of those three you are good to go for the kingdom of the Antichrist. This would easily cover everyone on earth. If you cannot or will not take the Mark you can use the name or the number of the name of the Antichrist to transact business. More advanced nations can take the mark for convenience. Lesser advanced nations or those lacking the RFID technology can simply take the name or number of the Antichrist. This means we do not need to wait for some advanced technology. We have everything right now for the rebellious to plug and play with the Antichrist.

Without the mark, name or number of the beast one cannot buy or sell. While the mark, name and number of the Beast certainly have economic privileges, the religious significance is far greater. This mark, name and number of the Beast is about professing religious allegiance to the Antichrist and his empire. Without this allegiance, you will not be able to buy or sell except in the underground markets. Notice how the Antichrist will control food distribution and use this as a snare to enslave people into his kingdom of darkness.

"And he causes all, both small and great, rich and poor, free and bond, to receive a mark in their right hand, or in their foreheads: And that **no man might buy or sell, save he that had the mark***, or the name of the beast, or the number of his name." Revelation 13:16-17*

13.2 - Don't Take the Mark, Name or Number of the Beast

We are also told that those accepting the mark of the beast will be cast into the lake of fire. As a new Christian, you must not accept the mark of the beast; it will doom you to the lake of fire. Stand strong in your profession of faith in Jesus even unto death. If someone tries to coerce or force you to take a chip, badge or identifying mark, then refuse it and run. Stay clear of places that issue the mark or that check people to ensure they have it. There could be checkpoints in cities and country roads, avoid them.

*"And the third angel followed them, saying with a loud voice, **If any man worship the beast and his image, and receive [his] mark in his forehead, or in his hand,** The same shall drink of the wine of the wrath of God, which is poured out without mixture into the cup of his indignation; and **he shall be tormented with fire and brimstone** in the presence of the holy angels, and in the presence of the Lamb: And the **smoke of their torment ascends up for ever and ever**: and they have no rest day nor night, who worship the beast and his image, and whosoever receives the mark of his name." Revelation 14:9-11*

This mark can be the RFID chip implant or a visible mark or item on the forehead or right arm. The mark will be something taken willingly by many people in the Middle East and throughout world. The meaning of the word translated mark is badge of servitude, branding or imprint. Remember, back in the first century there was no concept for implanting something in the skin.

Since we are talking about a Muslim Antichrist ruling over an Islamic Caliphate of 10 nations, the mark for Muslims could be the Muslim headband or armband that denotes allegiance to Islam. Fighters wear headbands and armbands showing allegiance to Islamic groups like Hamas and Hezbollah.

The Antichrist might alter the head and armbands to show allegiance to him and his Caliphate Empire. Since millions of Muslims are already wearing headbands this will be an easy and quick change. By wearing the headband, you are giving allegiance to the Antichrist and his kingdom. Don't' do it or your fate in hell is sealed.

Look for the Antichrist to implement this religious/commercial mark system in the second half of the seven-year tribulation. He must consolidate his power and control over the Islamic 10-nation Caliphate first. The rulers of the 10 nations will give the Antichrist power and authority for 3 ½ years.

This is my best understanding of the mark of the beast. However, it could be something else, something unforeseen at this writing. Whatever it may turn out to be, it will be mandatory for the Antichrist followers to have it. Stay alert, watch and see. Whatever it turns out to be just don't take it; keep your faith in Jesus Christ and do not become part of the evil system, the New World Order that is subduing the planet.

13.3 - Beware of Modern Bibles

Another interesting detail about the mark of the Beast is seen when observing the difference in the text between the King James Version and the modern bibles like the NIV. It pertains to the use of the words "in' and "on".

"And he causeth all, both small and great, rich and poor, free and bond, to receive a mark __in__ their right hand, or __in__ their foreheads:" - Revelation 13:16 KJV

"It also forced all people, great and small, rich and poor, free and slave, to receive a mark __on__ their right hands or __on__ their foreheads," - Revelation 13:16 NIV

People using the NIV can receive the RFID chip implant under the skin and still be in complete harmony with the text as it says "ON their right hands". On would be like a stamp or tattoo. NIV users could take the mark of the Beast and think they are still right with God and His word but end up in hell. The KJV users immediately understand that a chip implant is "in the right hand" and would not accept it thereby saving their souls from the lake of fire.

14 Trumpets of Woe

14.1 - A Book of Thirds

The Book of Revelation chapters 6 through 19 detail the events of the seven-year Tribulation. Many of these events are direct judgments from the Lord Jesus Christ sent upon earths unbelievers. These judgments appear in three sets; seven seals, seven trumpets and seven bowls. The first four seal judgments are referred to as the Four Horseman of the Apocalypse which we have already covered.

The fifth seal speaks of many martyrs for Christ. The sixth seal brings earthquakes and cosmic anomalies. These six seals occur during the first half of the Tribulation. Even though the judgments begin in sequential order their effects could last throughout the remaining years of the Tribulation.

14.2 - Fire, Hail and Blood

The seventh seal brings the seven trumpet judgments detailed in the Book of Revelation chapters 8 & 9. As you will see, these are partial judgment of thirds meant to be grave warnings and harbingers of what is to come. They are a call unto the world for repentance. The First Trumpet speaks of hail, fire and blood. A third of the grass and trees are consumed by fire. It is difficult to determine how only a third of the grass and trees are consumed.

But if you look at North and South America on a world map or globe, you see they make up about a third of the earth's land mass. Could something happen to the Americas that would completely wipe out both continents thereby consuming a third of the grass and trees. Food for thought. For example, what if a massive solar flare or coronal mass ejection hit the earth and the Americas happened to be facing the sun. North and South America would take the brunt of the destruction and the rest of the world would show little effect from the blast. So, that would account for the destruction by thirds.

*"The **first** angel sounded, and there followed **hail** and **fire** mingled with **blood**, and they were cast*

Pocket Guide to the Tribulation

*upon the earth: and the **third part of trees was burnt** up, and **all green grass was burnt up**."*
Revelation 8:7

14.3 - Enormous Volcano Eruption

The Second Trumpet judgment speaks of a burning mountain that is cast into the sea. This could be a massive volcanic eruption in the Middle East or the Mediterranean Sea area. There are many active volcanoes in the region so this is a distinct possibility. The profusion of the lava, ash and debris will turn the water red like blood.

Much of the sea life will die from the polluted water and many ships in the area will be destroyed. Mount Etna is a prime example of a large volcano located close to the Mediterranean waters. But this event reads like a Super Volcano eruption causing massive damage. You will know it when it happens as it will be devastating.

*"And the **second** angel sounded, and as it were a **great mountain burning with fire** was cast into the sea: and the third part of the sea became **blood**; And the third part of the creatures which were in the sea, and had life, died; and the third part of the ships were destroyed." - Revelation 8:8-9*

14.4 - Massive Meteor Strike

The Third Trumpet judgment tells of a star falling from heaven hitting the earth. This could easily be interpreted as a meteor hitting the earth

93

causing much destruction and polluting the fresh water supplies by a third. The star is named Wormwood which means "bitter or poison". This event is devastating and a great many people will die from the destruction and poison waters.

*"And the **third** angel sounded, and there fell a **great star from heaven, burning as it were a lamp**, and it fell upon the third part of the rivers, and upon the fountains of waters; And the name of the star is called Wormwood: and the third part of the waters became wormwood; and many men died of the waters, because they were made bitter." - Revelation 8:10-11*

14.5 - Atmospheric Effluence

The Fourth Trumpet judgment finds the atmosphere filled with so much dust, smoke and ash that the sun, moon and stars are darkened. This is not a good thing as temperatures could drop, and oxygen production from the oceans could be reduced having yet another devastating effect on all life on earth.

*"And the **fourth** angel sounded, and the third part of the **sun** was smitten, and the third part of the **moon**, and the third part of the **stars**; so as the third part of them was **darkened**, and the day shone not for a third part of it, and the night likewise." - Revelation 8:12*

14.6 - Woe, Woe, Woe

It gets real interesting here as the last three trumpets are placed in a worse category of pain and destruction. They are called "woes" meaning a primary interjection of pain and grief. The fifth angel's trumpet brings a woe of pain and suffering to each and every person that has taken the mark of the beast. A stinging locust/scorpion like creature is released upon earth to torment those following the Antichrist. Only those that have taken the mark of the beast will feel the scorpion sting.

The sting's pain lasts for 5 months but does not kill anyone, only torments Antichrist's followers. These demonic creatures are very bizarre as described in the following Scripture text. They are unlike anything the earth has seen so they should be easy to identify when they arrive. Oh, not to worry, if you are a true follower of Jesus Christ they won't bother you. They only torment Antichrist and his followers; some long overdue payback.

14.7 - Locust Anomaly

*"And the **fifth** angel sounded, and I saw a star fall from heaven unto the earth: and to him was given the key of the bottomless pit. And he opened the bottomless pit; and there arose a smoke out of the pit, as the smoke of a great furnace; and the sun and the air were darkened by reason of the smoke of the pit. And there came out of the smoke **locusts upon the earth**: and unto them was given power, as the scorpions of the*

earth have power. And it was commanded them that they should not hurt the grass of the earth, neither any green thing, neither any tree; but only those men which have not the seal of God in their foreheads. And to them it was given that they should not kill them, but that they should be tormented five months: and their torment [was] as the torment of a scorpion, when he striketh a man. And in those days shall men seek death, and shall not find it; and shall desire to die, and death shall flee from them. And the shapes of the locusts [were] like unto horses prepared unto battle; and on their heads [were] as it were crowns like gold, and their faces [were] as the faces of men. And they had hair as the hair of women, and their teeth were as [the teeth] of lions. And they had breastplates, as it were breastplates of iron; and the sound of their wings [was] as the sound of chariots of many horses running to battle. **And they had tails like unto scorpions, and there were stings in their tails: and their power [was] to hurt men five months.** *And they had a king over them, [which is] the angel of the bottomless pit, whose name in the Hebrew tongue [is] Abaddon, but in the Greek tongue hath [his] name Apollyon. One woe is past; [and], behold, there come two woes more hereafter." - Revelation 9:1-12*

Wow, bizarre beyond words. Demonic scorpion like locusts arise from the bottomless pit and torment everyone for five months. Everyone except those having God's seal in their foreheads. These stinging locusts are not allowed to kill anyone, only torment. They have a ruler, the king

Pocket Guide to the Tribulation

of the bottomless pit. His name is Apollyon /Abaddon which means the destroyer. This nightmare scenario lasts for five long months.

14.8 - Armies from the East

The sixth trumpet is the second woe. There is an appointed time when an army of 200 million men, creatures or something is released from the East and cross the Euphrates River in Iraq. This Satanic army will unleash such unheard-of death and destruction that one third of the population is killed. That brings the death toll on planet earth to one half; 4 billion people. Here again we have a description of something very bizarre. The numbers are so large one cannot imagine such a scenario. Even the Hollywood Epics will pale into insignificance. One thing is for certain, you will not miss them when they are gathered. 200 million of anything is pretty hard to miss.

*"And the **sixth** angel sounded, and I heard a voice from the four horns of the golden altar which is before God, Saying to the sixth angel which had the trumpet, Loose the four angels which are bound in the great river Euphrates. And the four angels were loosed, which were prepared for an hour, and a day, and a month, and a year, for to slay the third part of men. And the number of the army of the horsemen [were] **two hundred thousand thousand**: and I heard the number of them. And thus I saw the horses in the vision, and them that sat on them, having breastplates of fire,*

and of jacinth, and brimstone: and the heads of the horses [were] as the heads of lions; and out of their mouths issued fire and smoke and brimstone. **By these three was the third part of men killed, by the fire, and by the smoke, and by the brimstone, which issued out of their mouths**. *For their power is in their mouth, and in their tails: for their tails [were] like unto serpents, and had heads, and with them they do hurt. And the rest of the men which were not killed by these plagues yet repented not of the works of their hands, that they should not worship devils, and idols of gold, and silver, and brass, and stone, and of wood: which neither can see, nor hear, nor walk: Neither repented they of their murders, nor of their sorceries, nor of their fornication, nor of their thefts." - Revelation 9:13-21*

These judgments are intended to make things so bad that people will repent of their sins and turn to God. However, most do not repent and continue in their sin and rebellion.

Many of the judgments of God are difficult to explain but one thing is for sure. As these judgments draw near, clues from current events will bring light to these prophetic scriptures. Keep your heart, mind and eye open to the Word of God.

15 Bowls of Wrath

15.1 - Pure Wrath

The Bowl judgments occur close to the end of the Tribulation. They are the seven last plagues from God listed in Revelation Ch. 16. These bowls or vials symbolically contain the concentrated wrath of God that will be poured out upon the earth.

15.2 - Nasty Open Sores

The first bowl of wrath is a nasty foul sore that befalls all those that took the mark of the beast. We are not talking about a little zit but a repugnant, repulsive, horrible, almost debilitating open wound or abscess; and not just one but many. The fact that this nasty sore only comes upon those that took the mark of the beast gives credence to the idea that the mark is some sort of skin implant which yields a very bad reaction resulting in the sores. Remember, don't take the mark of the beast, no matter how convenient it may seem or how "Hollywood" the marketing campaign may be.

*"And the **first** went, and poured out his vial upon the earth; and there fell a **noisome and grievous sore** upon the men which had the mark of the beast, and [upon] them which worshipped his image." - Revelation 16:2*

99

15.3 - Salt Water Blood Soup

The second bowl of wrath seems to be a completion of the second trumpet judgment where one third of the waters were turned to blood. Now the entire sea becomes as the blood of a dead man. That is pretty gross as the blood of a dead man is coagulated blood. I don't even want to think about it. Is this referring to the Dead Sea, the Sea of Galilee, the Mediterranean Sea or all the sea? Not sure, the word sea can have a local or global context. We know that this plague is for bodies of salt water as the next bowl is for fresh water rivers. However, this plays out it is disastrous for mankind.

*"And the **second** angel poured out his vial upon the **sea**; and it became as the **blood of a dead [man]**: and every living soul **died** in the sea." - Revelation 16:3*

15.4 - Foul Fresh Water

The third bowl of wrath is similar to the second. However, this judgment is for fresh water rivers and lakes. These bodies of water are the primary supply of drinking water for mankind. With water supplies diminished many deaths will result. The Fourth Horseman, the pale green horse of Death and Hell is very busy as millions upon millions die. This is a righteous judgment from the Lord upon the unbelievers as they have martyred many Christians and now they are given blood to drink. Fear not, if you are a believer in Jesus Christ know that these things must come to pass but God will take care of His own.

*"And the **third** angel poured out his vial upon the **rivers and fountains of waters**; and they became **blood**. And I heard the angel of the waters say, Thou art righteous, O Lord, which art, and wast, and shalt be, because thou hast judged thus. **For they have shed the blood of saints and prophets, and thou hast given them blood to drink**; for they are worthy. And I heard another out of the altar say, Even so, Lord God Almighty, true and righteous [are] thy judgments." - Revelation 16:4-7*

15.5 - Burn Baby Burn

The fourth bowl of wrath concerns the sun. Something happens with our sun that results in a significant increase in heat. This increase in intensity brings fires upon the earth. We have in the past seen very large fires in western states and Alaska. The fires to come during the last days of the Tribulation will make anything heretofore pale into insignificance. This will not be just forest fires but cities will burn. Many will die from the heat and the fires. I feel like I am repeating myself; many will die from this or that. But it is true, at least half the population of the planet will die; 4+ BILLION people because they would not repent and believe in Jesus Christ.

Pocket Guide to the Tribulation

*"And the **fourth** angel poured out his vial upon the **sun**; and power was given unto him to scorch men with **fire**. And men were **scorched with great heat**, and **blasphemed the name of God**, which hath power over these plagues: and they repented not to give him glory."* - Revelation 16:8-9

I remember when I was young the sun was yellow. Even in school we drew a yellow sun. But now the sun seems white. Scientists are realizing our sun is not the stable star they once thought. When I was young the light from the sun was softer. Now it seems harsh and penetrating. Maybe it's just me but I think the sun has changed even in my lifetime.

15.6 - Doom and Gloom

The fifth bowl of wrath is poured directly upon the Kingdom of the Antichrist. His seat of power is Jerusalem. This seems to be primarily directed at the Middle East as the Antichrist kingdom is centered in the Middle East. The "darkness" poured upon his kingdom is not just a physical darkness but a spiritual darkness. Perhaps some of you reading this book have experienced a spiritual heaviness, an evil oppression of mind and soul. During the Tribulation, the demonic and satanic oppression will be so thick and heavy you can cut it with a knife. A great many will not be able to handle this and will seek their own death.

Instead of repenting of their sin and seeking the Lord, they blaspheme and suffer, sealing their fate in hell.

> *"And the **fifth** angel poured out his vial upon the **seat of the beast**; and his kingdom was **full of darkness**; and they gnawed their tongues for pain, And blasphemed the God of heaven because of their pains and their sores, and repented not of their deeds." - Revelation 16:10-11*

15.7 - Get Ready for Armageddon

With the sixth bowl of wrath we are getting close to the final battle, the Battle of Armageddon. This bowl dries up the Euphrates River and probably the Tigris also so the armies of the world can gather in Israel. The armies gather in northern Israel from the valley of Jezreel to Mount Megiddo for this last great battle. The purpose of this battle is not to conquer Israel; that has already happened in the middle of the seven years when the Antichrist perpetrates the Abomination of Desolation spoken of in prior chapters.

The purpose of this battle is to prevent Jesus from returning to earth and setting up His Kingdom. Satan wants to rule the earth for a thousand years through his puppet the Antichrist. He will muster his armies in a futile attempt to prevent the second coming of Jesus Christ. Can you imagine anything so preposterous, so arrogant, so narcissistic?

Pocket Guide to the Tribulation

"And the **sixth** *angel poured out his vial upon the* **great river Euphrates**; *and the water thereof was* **dried up**, *that the way of the kings of the east might be prepared. And I saw three unclean spirits like frogs [come] out of the mouth of the dragon, and out of the mouth of the beast, and out of the mouth of the false prophet. For they are the spirits of devils, working miracles, [which] go forth unto the kings of the earth and of the whole world,* **to gather them to the battle of that great day of God Almighty**. *Behold, I come as a thief. Blessed [is] he that watcheth, and keepeth his garments, lest he walk naked, and they see his shame.* **And he gathered them together into a place called in the Hebrew tongue Armageddon**." - *Revelation 16:12-16*

15.8 - What the Hail

The seventh bowl of wrath is a grand finale earthquake that shakes the entire planet. This earthquake is so massive that cities around the world are destroyed, islands will vanish back into the sea and mountains will fall like a house of cards. This earthquake will reshape the surface of the earth in preparation for the thousand-year reign of the Lord Jesus Christ. Everything will be affected by the earthquake and the great hailstones. Can you imagine hail weighing 70 to 100 pounds? That is the weight of a talent. Hailstones of this magnitude will destroy everything they hit. Little will survive the destructive power of this gigantic hail and massive earthquake.

Pocket Guide to the Tribulation

All the works of men will be destroyed and the earth will be remade as Jesus desires according to His wonderful plans. The angel proclaims "It is done". The wrath of God on a blasphemous Antichrist kingdom is finished. The final battle is next.

> "And the **seventh** angel poured out his vial into the air; and there came a great voice out of the temple of heaven, from the throne, saying, **It is done**. And there were voices, and thunders, and lightnings; and there was **a great earthquake**, such as was not since men were upon the earth, so mighty an earthquake, [and] so great. And the great city was divided into three parts, and the **cities of the nations fell**: and great Babylon came in remembrance before God, to give unto her the cup of the wine of the fierceness of his wrath. And **every island fled away, and the mountains were not found**. And there fell upon men a **great hail out of heaven**, [every stone] about the weight of a talent: and men blasphemed God because of the plague of the hail; for the plague thereof was exceeding great." - Revelation 16:17-21

These trumpet and bowl (vial) judgments are very horrific and catastrophic. Some are easier to understand than others. For example, in the trumpet judgments, a burning mountain is probably a volcano; a star fall from heaven could be a meteor making some water sources poison; the sun, moon and stars smitten by 1/3 could be dust and ash in the atmosphere blocking the light.

However, demonic locust like creatures, you'll have to wait and see that one. Keep your eyes open so you will recognize each of these judgments as they happen. They will be difficult to miss. But most will not understand what is happening. Remember, the Apostle John was trying to explain 21st century events in 1st century lingo. Nothing in his day could describe nuclear weapons, fighter jets, battle tanks, apache helicopters and a host of other modern implements.

The bowl judgments seem to be directed at the Antichrist, his kingdom and followers. They affect those having the mark of the beast, the Antichrists seat of power, the sea and water supplies in the Middle East and the Euphrates River. It is my opinion that some of these judgments will have global consequences. Hunker down, watch and be prepared, your redemption is near. Jesus is coming soon. The last bowl judgment occurs immediately before the battle of Armageddon so it's almost over.

16 The Battle of Armageddon

16.1 - The Mother of All Battles

The Battle of Armageddon is fought at the end of the seven-year Tribulation. The location is the valley of Jezreel/Megiddo in north central Israel.

As you can see, this is the perfect place for a war as the entire valley can be seen from the surrounding hills. The valley stretches about 60 miles, beginning at the Mediterranean coast moving southeast to the Jordan River.

However, the plane of Megiddo above might be the staging area for the final battle of the Tribulation. The Lord gathers the Antichrist armies to this plane in preparation for the battle over who

107

will reign in Jerusalem. The city will be attacked and half of the city will be taken. Then the Lord returns to fight for His people the Jews.

*"Behold, the day of the LORD cometh, and thy spoil shall be divided in the midst of thee. For **I will gather all nations against Jerusalem to battle***; *and the city shall be taken, and the houses rifled, and the women ravished; and half of the city shall go forth into captivity, and the residue of the people shall not be cut off from the city. Then shall the LORD go forth, and fight against those nations, as when he fought in the day of battle." - Zechariah 14:1-3*

16.2 - Battle over the Kingdom

This war over Jerusalem will involve many nations. The Prophet Ezekiel tells us the invading armies include Turkey, Persia (Iran, Afghanistan and Pakistan), Sudan, Libya and others. The Prophet Jeremiah includes Egypt, Gaza, Jordan, Lebanon, Saudi Arabia, Iraq, and Syria. This final war will see the use of nuclear weapons. The Bible calls this a plague where peoples tongues will be burned out of their mouths and their eyes will be consumed from their sockets before their bodies can fall to the ground.

"And this shall be the plague wherewith the LORD will smite all the people that have fought against Jerusalem; Their flesh shall consume away while they stand upon their feet, and their eyes shall consume

108

away in their holes, and their tongue shall consume away in their mouth." - Zechariah 14:12

Prior the nuclear age there was no way for this to happen. But this is the exact effect of the neutron bomb. Where the nuclear exchange takes place in the Middle East is not precisely mentioned. However, there is a prophecy that Damascus Syria will be turned into a desolate ruin. I would also expect one to hit Israel, Jordan and Arabia.

This will be a time of horrific terror for most people but be calm, all this must happen; Jesus is coming soon. As the end of the seven-year Tribulation approaches, be ready and keep watching for your deliverance is drawing near.

Even though the battle of Armageddon is over Jerusalem, the true purpose, from the Antichrists perspective, is to prevent the second coming of Jesus Christ. Of course, this is a fool's endeavor. These massive armies gathering to prevent Jesus from returning and setting up His Millennial Kingdom are easily defeated by the Lord Jesus Christ.

"And I saw the beast, and the kings of the earth, and their armies, gathered together to make war against him that sat on the horse, and against his army." - Revelation 19:19

Pocket Guide to the Tribulation

17 Gog Magog War

17.1 - Ezekiel's View

I want to address this portion of Bible prophecy as it speaks to a great war in the Last Days. These two chapters in the book of Ezekiel are very descriptive but controversy over the timing of this war persists. Some say it happens before the Tribulation, some say in the Middle and others place it at the end of the seven years synonymous with the Battle of Armageddon. That is why I have placed it here in the chapter on the Battle of Armageddon, as I believe that the Gog-Magog war is Armageddon just seen from Ezekiel's perspective.

Keep in mind that Armageddon is the great battle at the end of the seven-year Tribulation while the Gog war is a broader war that takes much longer to play out. I believe that the battle of Armageddon is the final battle of the Gog-Magog war. There are many similarities I will note as we proceed with this study.

*"And the word of the LORD came unto me, saying, Son of man, set thy face **against Gog, the land of Magog, the chief prince of Meshech and Tubal**, and prophesy against him, And say, Thus saith the Lord GOD; Behold, I [am] against thee, O Gog, the chief prince of Meshech and Tubal:" - Ezekiel 38:1-3*

Pocket Guide to the Tribulation

17.2 - The Main Players

The prophecy is against someone referred to as Gog from the land of Magog. Gog is also the chief prince of Meshech and Tubal. Very little is known about Gog. This could be a reference to King Gogez that ruled the Turkic tribes in Asia Minor during the 7th century B.C. around the time of the prophet Ezekiel. However, we do know something about Magog. He was the grandson of Noah and settled in Asia Minor after Noah's flood. Magog settled the area of Armenia in eastern Turkey. Meshech, Tubal, Gomer and Togarmah are also located in central Asia Minor, modern day Turkey.

"Persia, Ethiopia, and Libya with them; all of them with shield and helmet: Gomer, and all his bands; the house of Togarmah of the north quarters, and all his bands: [and] many people with thee." - Ezekiel 38:5-6

The modern-day nations that make up this coalition are Turkey, Iran (Persia), Sudan (Ethiopia) and Libya. We could include the countries of Afghanistan and Pakistan since they were part of ancient Persia. So, it is easy to see that these are all Middle Eastern Muslim nations. Some want to include Russia and that might be possible as many others are part of this coalition.

*"After many days thou shalt be visited: in the **latter years** thou shalt come into the land [that is]*

Pocket Guide to the Tribulation

*brought back from the sword, [and is] gathered out of many people, **against the mountains of Israel**, which have been always waste: but it is brought forth out of the nations, and they shall dwell safely all of them." - Ezekiel 38:8*

17.3 - Spoil, Soil and Oil

In the latter days, this coalition of nations will invade Israel. Historically these nations have never joined together to invade Israel so this must be yet future as of this writing. The reason for this invasion is to take a spoil, to take land, resources and goods. Israel has resources of natural gas, oil and food. These are valuable commodities and will be of great value during the Tribulation.

*"To take **a spoil**, and to take **a prey**; to turn thine hand upon the desolate places [that are now] inhabited, and upon the people [that are] gathered out of the nations, which have gotten cattle and goods, that dwell in the midst of the land." - Ezekiel 38:12*

Needless to say, this invasion of Israel makes God furious and full of anger. He is jealous for His people and the fire of His wrath is unleashed. A great shaking occurs in Israel possibly a global earthquake affecting both land and sea. Seems that everything and everyone is affected. Everything will shake at the presence of the Lord. Mountains will fall as we have read about in the judgments of the Book of revelation.

17.4 - God's Great Weapons

"And it shall come to pass at the same time when Gog shall come against the land of Israel, saith the Lord GOD, [that] my fury shall come up in my face. For in my jealousy [and] in the fire of my wrath have I spoken, Surely in that day there shall be a great shaking in the land of Israel; So that the fishes of the sea, and the fowls of the heaven, and the beasts of the field, and all creeping things that creep upon the earth, and all the men that [are] upon the face of the earth, shall shake at my presence, and the mountains shall be thrown down, and the steep places shall fall, and every wall shall fall to the ground." - Ezekiel 38:18-20

The Lord will bring pestilence, blood, rain, fire and great hailstones against Gog, the Antichrist. This again sounds very similar to language used in describing the trumpet and bowl judgments from the Book of Revelation.

*"And I will plead against him with **pestilence** and with **blood**; and I will **rain** upon him, and upon his bands, and upon the many people that [are] with him, an overflowing rain, and **great hailstones**, **fire**, and **brimstone**." - Ezekiel 38:22*

17.5 - Nuclear Exchange

The Lord will destroy most of Gog's army leaving only one sixth alive. It will take seven years to dispose of all the weapons captured or destroyed in the war. Many will die in this war and a giant graveyard will be built east of the Dead Sea.

*"And they shall sever out **men of continual employment**, passing through the land to bury with the passengers those that remain upon the face of the earth, **to cleanse it**: after the end of seven months shall they search. And the passengers [that] pass through the land, when [any] **seeth a man's bone**, then shall he **set up a sign by it**, till the buriers have buried it in the valley of Hamongog." - Ezekiel 39:14-15*

This language sounds like a HAZMAT team going through the land to dispose of any dead bodies or body parts possibly resulting from a nuclear weapon explosion.

17.6 - God's Great Feast

*"And, thou son of man, thus saith the Lord GOD; Speak unto **every feathered fowl**, and to every **beast of the field**, Assemble yourselves, and come; gather yourselves on every side to **my sacrifice** that I do sacrifice for you, [even] a great sacrifice upon the mountains of Israel, that ye may **eat flesh**, and **drink blood.** Ye shall eat **the flesh of the mighty**, and drink the **blood of the princes** of the earth, of rams, of lambs, and of goats, of bullocks, all of them fatlings of Bashan. And ye shall eat fat till ye be full, and drink blood till ye be drunken, of **my sacrifice which I have sacrificed for you**. Thus ye shall be filled at my table with horses and chariots, with mighty men, and*

with all men of war, saith the Lord GOD." - Ezekiel 39:17-20

Wow, a great slaughter and sacrifice of Gog's armies given to the birds and the beasts. This sounds very much like the language in the Book of Revelation describing the aftermath of the Battle of Armageddon.

*"And I saw an angel standing in the sun; and he cried with a loud voice, saying to **all the fowls that fly in the midst of heaven**, Come and gather yourselves together unto the **supper of the great God**; That ye may **eat the flesh of kings**, and the **flesh of captains**, and the **flesh of mighty men**, and the **flesh of horses**, and of them that sit on them, and the flesh of all [men, both] free and bond, both small and great." - Revelation 19:17-18*

17.7 - The Lord in Israel

The final result of this great war of Gog is that Israel will know and believe that Jesus is their Messiah. They will then accept their rightful King their ancestors crucified.

*"Then shall they know that **I [am] the LORD their God**, which caused them to be led into captivity among the heathen: but **I have gathered them unto their own land**, and have left none of them anymore there. Neither will I hide my face any more from them:*

*for **I have poured out my spirit upon the house
of Israel**, saith the Lord GOD." - Ezekiel 39:28-29*

It is my opinion that the Battle of
Armageddon is the culmination of the Gog-Magog
war. This war could start at the middle of the
Tribulation when the Antichrist takes Jerusalem
and the Temple. However it plays out, the Gog-
Magog war begins before the Battle of Armageddon.

18 The Second Coming of Jesus Christ

18.1 - The King of Kings

The long seven years is coming to a close. The Battle of Armageddon is on. The catastrophic judgments of God are finished. The conditions on the earth are horrific and hundreds of millions of people have died. In general, most people are not looking for the Lord Jesus Christ to return, they are just trying to survive. As we have noted earlier, He comes as a thief in the night. His return will be a surprise to most because they do not believe Bible prophecy.

"For as the lightning cometh out of the east, and shineth even unto the west; so shall also the coming of the Son of man be." - Matthew 24:27

However, you know the truth. As the time approaches, be looking for the Lord to return to Jerusalem. He will in fact return to the Mount of Olives just east of Jerusalem and the Temple Mount.

"Then shall the LORD go forth, and fight against those nations, as when he fought in the day of battle. ***And his feet shall stand in that day upon the mount of Olives****, which [is] before Jerusalem on the east, and the mount of Olives shall cleave in the midst thereof toward the east and toward the west, [and there shall be] a very great valley; and half of the mountain shall remove toward the north, and half of it toward the south." - Zechariah 14:3-4*

The Mount of Olives is covered with graves. A lot of folks plan on being resurrected at the return of Jesus so what better place.

The Book of Revelation pictures the Lord Jesus leaving heaven riding on a white horse bringing judgment and war. His eyes are as flames of fire and He is wearing many crowns. He is called Faithful and True, the Word of God.

> *"And I saw heaven opened, and behold a **white horse**; and he that sat upon him [was] called **Faithful and True**, and in righteousness he **doth judge and make war**. His eyes [were] as a flame of fire, and on his head [were] many crowns; and he had a name written, that no man knew, but he himself. And he [was] clothed with a vesture dipped in blood: and his name is called **The Word of God**." - Revelation 19:11-13*

18.2 - The Saints Go Marching In

His army follows Him also riding on white horses. These are the saints of the Lord that were raptured seven years ago. Can you imagine the shock and awe factor to a follower of the Antichrist looking up and seeing millions of warriors on white horses coming from the clouds of heaven heading in your direction?

> *"And the armies [which were] in heaven followed him upon white horses, clothed in fine linen, white and clean. And he hath on [his] vesture and on his thigh a name written, **KING OF KINGS, AND LORD OF LORDS**. - Revelation 19:14-16*

This will be a glorious day as you finally meet in person your Lord and Savior Jesus Christ. Your eternal destiny is now secure in Jesus and you will enter His Millennial Kingdom. Let the holy celebration begin. I will see you there my friend. Please look me up after things calm down, I would love to meet you and hear your story. God Bless and keep the faith.

18.3 - Satan Bound

After Jesus returns he sends forth an angel to capture Satan, put him in chains and lock him in the bottomless pit. He is chained there for one thousand years. That is the timeframe of the first part of Jesus Christ's Kingdom here on earth.

*"And I saw an angel come down from heaven, having the **key of the bottomless pit and a great chain** in his hand. And he laid hold on the dragon, that old serpent, which is the Devil, and Satan, and **bound him a thousand years**, And cast him into the bottomless pit, and shut him up, and set a seal upon him, that he should deceive the nations no more, till the thousand years should be fulfilled: and after that he must be loosed a little season." - Revelation 20:1-3 KJV*

Interesting that after the one thousand years Satan is loosed from his chains and released from the bottomless pit for a "little season". I will talk more about that in a subsequent chapter.

19   Jesus Christ, Man of War

Most do not picture Jesus Christ as a man of war. He is thought of as a moral teacher, an example of ethical behavior or simply a good man. Even most Christians think of Him only as loving, compassionate and righteous. He is certainly all that and much more. But in the Book of Revelation we see Jesus as one resembling the Old Testament Lord of hosts, Captain of heaven's armies.

"And I saw heaven opened, and behold a white horse; and he that sat upon him [was] called Faithful and True, and in righteousness he doth judge and **make war.***" - Revelation 19:11 KJV*

Make war; yes, make war.   Jesus is returning at the end of the seven-year Tribulation to make war with the armies of the Antichrist that are trying to prevent His return. Fighting against Jesus is futile as He defeats them handily.   As He sets up His Kingdom, those nations that step out of line will feel the rod of iron with which He rules.

"And out of his mouth goeth a sharp sword, that with it he should **smite the nations***: and he shall rule them with a* **rod of iron***: and he* **treadeth the**

winepress *of the fierceness and wrath of Almighty God." - Revelation 19:15 KJV*

The symbolic winepress that Jesus treads is not full of grapes; it is full of His enemies. The armies of earth are in the winepress and Jesus is treading them out. Blood comes from the winepress flowing several feet deep for 200 miles; 1600 furlongs.

*"And the angel thrust in his sickle into the earth, and gathered the vine of the earth, and cast [it] into the **great winepress of the wrath of God**. And the winepress was trodden without the city, and **blood came out of the winepress**, even unto the horse bridles, by the space of a thousand [and] six hundred furlongs." - Revelation 14:19-20 KJV*

There is a very interesting verse in Isaiah Ch. 63 as follows:

*"Who [is] this that cometh from Edom, with dyed garments from Bozrah? this [that is] glorious in his apparel, travelling in the greatness of his strength? I that speak in righteousness, mighty to save. **Wherefore [art thou] red in thine apparel**, and thy garments like him that treadeth in the winefat? I have **trodden the winepress** alone; and of the people [there was] none with me: for I will tread them in **mine anger,** and trample them in **my fury**; and **their blood shall be sprinkled upon my garments**, and I will stain all my raiment. For the day of vengeance*

124

[is] in mine heart, and the year of my redeemed is come." - Isaiah 63:1-4 KJV

Jesus is returning from doing battle in Jordan (Bozrah, Edom) with the blood of His enemies on His garments. He crushes them in the winepress of His anger and fury, staining His cloths red with their blood. The day of the Lord's vengeance has fully come.

20 The Day of the Lord

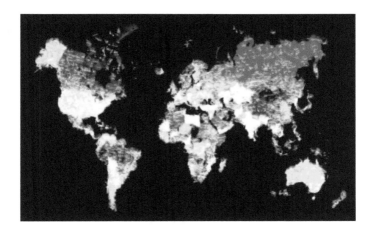

20.1 - A Day of Thick Darkness

The Day of the Lord scriptures are numerous in the Old Testament. They describe events and conditions leading up to the return of Jesus Christ. I have discussed this timeframe throughout this book and included many scripture texts. The following is a compilation of Day of the Lord Scripture verses. They paint a pretty dark and gloomy time for folks on earth that have missed the Rapture and are left behind. Also, there are verses that give hope to those who have received Jesus Christ as Lord and Savior during the Tribulation.

*"For the **day of the LORD** of hosts shall be upon every one that is proud and lofty, and upon every one that is lifted up; and he shall be brought low:"* - Isaiah 2:12

*"Howl ye; for the **day of the LORD** is at hand; it shall come as a destruction from the Almighty. ... Behold, the **day of the LORD** cometh, cruel both with wrath and fierce anger, to lay the land desolate: and he shall destroy the sinners thereof out of it."* - Isaiah 13:6, 9

*"For it is the **day of the LORD'S** vengeance, and the year of recompenses for the controversy of Zion."* - Isaiah 34:8

*"For this is the **day of the Lord** GOD of hosts, a day of vengeance, that he may avenge him of his adversaries: and the sword shall devour, and it shall be satiate and made drunk with their blood: for the Lord GOD of hosts hath a sacrifice in the north country by the river Euphrates."* - Jeremiah 46:10

*"Thou hast called as in a solemn day my terrors round about, so that in the **day of the LORD'S** anger none escaped nor remained: those that I have swaddled and brought up hath mine enemy consumed."* - Lamentations 2:22

*"For the day is near, even the **day of the LORD** is near, a cloudy day; it shall be the time of the heathen."* - Ezekiel 30:3

*"Alas for the day! for the **day of the LORD** is at hand, and as a destruction from the Almighty shall it come." - Joel 1:15*

*"Blow ye the trumpet in Zion, and sound an alarm in my holy mountain: let all the inhabitants of the land tremble: for the **day of the LORD** cometh, for it is nigh at hand; ... And the LORD shall utter his voice before his army: for his camp is very great: for he is strong that executes his word: for the **day of the LORD** is great and very terrible; and who can abide it? ... The sun shall be turned into darkness, and the moon into blood, before the great and the terrible **day of the LORD** come." - Joel 2:1, 11, 31*

*"Multitudes, multitudes in the valley of decision: for the **day of the LORD** is near in the valley of decision." - Joel 3:14*

*"Woe unto you that desire the **day of the LORD**! to what end is it for you? the **day of the LORD** is darkness, and not light. ... Shall not the **day of the LORD** be darkness, and not light? even very dark, and no brightness in it?" - Amos 5:18, 20*

*"For the **day of the LORD** is near upon all the heathen: as thou hast done, it shall be done unto thee: thy reward shall return upon thine own head." - Obadiah 1:15*

*"Hold thy peace at the presence of the Lord GOD: for **the day of the LORD** is at hand: for the LORD hath **prepared a sacrifice**, he hath bid his guests. And it shall come to pass in the **day of the***

LORD'S sacrifice, that I will punish the princes, and the king's children, and all such as are clothed with strange apparel. ... The great **day of the LORD** is near, it is near, and hasteth greatly, even the voice of the **day of the LORD**: the mighty man shall cry there bitterly. ... Neither their silver nor their gold shall be able to deliver them in the **day of the LORD'S** wrath; but the whole land shall be devoured by the fire of his jealousy: for he shall make even a speedy riddance of all them that dwell in the land." - Zephaniah 1:7-8, 14, 18

"Before the decree bring forth, before the day pass as the chaff, before the fierce anger of the LORD come upon you, before the **day of the LORD'S** anger come upon you. Seek ye the LORD, all ye meek of the earth, which have wrought his judgment; seek righteousness, seek meekness: it may be ye shall be hid in the **day of the LORD'S** anger." - Zephaniah 2:2-3

"Behold, the **day of the LORD** cometh, and thy spoil shall be divided in the midst of thee." - Zechariah 14:1

"Behold, I will send you Elijah the prophet before the coming of the great and dreadful **day of the LORD:**" - Malachi 4:5

"For yourselves know perfectly that the **day of the Lord** so cometh as a thief in the night." - 1 Thessalonians 5:2

*"But the **day of the Lord** will come as a thief in the night; in the which the heavens shall pass away with a great noise, and the elements shall melt with fervent heat, the earth also and the works that are therein shall be burned up." - 2 Peter 3:10*

20.2 - Oh, That Day

There are many verses that refer to the Day of the Lord simply as "that day"; below is just a sample.

*"The lofty looks of man shall be humbled, and the haughtiness of men shall be bowed down, and the LORD alone shall be exalted in that day. ... And the loftiness of man shall be bowed down, and the haughtiness of men shall be made low: and the LORD alone shall be exalted in that day. ... In **that day** a man shall cast his idols of silver, and his idols of gold, which they made each one for himself to worship, to the moles and to the bats;" - Isaiah 2:11, 17, 20*

*"And in **that day** they shall roar against them like the roaring of the sea: and if one look unto the land, behold darkness and sorrow, and the light is darkened in the heavens thereof." - Isaiah 5:30*

*"And it shall come to pass in **that day**, that the Lord shall set his hand again the second time to recover the remnant of his people, which shall be left, from Assyria, and from Egypt, and from Pathros, and from Cush, and from Elam, and from Shinar, and from Hamath, and from the islands of the sea." - Isaiah 11:11*

Pocket Guide to the Tribulation

"And in **that day** thou shalt say, O LORD, I will praise thee: though thou wast angry with me, thine anger is turned away, and thou comforted me. ... And in **that day** shall ye say, Praise the LORD, call upon his name, declare his doings among the people, make mention that his name is exalted." - Isaiah 12:1, 4

"In **that day** shall his strong cities be as a forsaken bough, and an uppermost branch, which they left because of the children of Israel: and there shall be desolation." - Isaiah 17:9

"In **that day** shall Egypt be like unto women: and it shall be afraid and fear because of the shaking of the hand of the LORD of hosts, which he shaketh over it." - Isaiah 19:16

"And it shall come to pass in **that day**, that the LORD shall punish the host of the high ones that are on high, and the kings of the earth upon the earth." - Isaiah 24:21

"And it shall be said in **that day**, Lo, this is our God; we have waited for him, and he will save us: this is the LORD; we have waited for him, we will be glad and rejoice in his salvation." - Isaiah 25:9

"In **that day** the LORD with his sore and great and strong sword shall punish leviathan the piercing serpent, even leviathan that crooked serpent; and he shall slay the dragon that is in the sea. ... And it shall come to pass in **that day**, that the great trumpet shall be blown, and they shall come which were ready to *perish in the land of Assyria, and the outcasts in the land of Egypt, and shall worship the LORD in the holy mount at Jerusalem." - Isaiah 27:1, 13*

*"In **that day** shall the LORD of hosts be for a crown of glory, and for a diadem of beauty, unto the residue of his people," - Isaiah 28:5*

*"And the slain of the LORD shall be at **that day** from one end of the earth even unto the other end of the earth: they shall not be lamented, neither gathered, nor buried; they shall be dung upon the ground." - Jeremiah 25:33*

*"Alas! for **that day** is great, so that none is like it: it is even the time of Jacob's trouble; but he shall be saved out of it. For it shall come to pass in **that day**, saith the LORD of hosts, that I will break his yoke from off thy neck, and will burst thy bonds, and strangers shall no more serve themselves of him:" - Jeremiah 30:7-8*

*"Behold, he shall come up and fly as the eagle, and spread his wings over Bozrah: and at **that day** shall the heart of the mighty men of Edom be as the heart of a woman in her pangs." - Jeremiah 49:22*

*"For in my jealousy and in the fire of my wrath have I spoken, Surely in **that day** there shall be a great shaking in the land of Israel;" - Ezekiel 38:19*

*"And it shall come to pass in **that day**, that the mountains shall drop down new wine, and the hills shall flow with milk, and all the rivers of Judah shall*

flow with waters, and a fountain shall come forth of the house of the LORD, and shall water the valley of Shittim." - Joel 3:18

*"And it shall come to pass in **that day**, saith the Lord GOD, that I will cause the sun to go down at noon, and I will darken the earth in the clear day:" - Amos 8:9*

*"**That day** is a day of wrath, a day of trouble and distress, a day of wasteness and desolation, a day of darkness and gloominess, a day of clouds and thick darkness," - Zephaniah 1:15*

*"And in **that day** will I make Jerusalem a burdensome stone for all people: all that burden themselves with it shall be cut in pieces, though all the people of the earth be gathered together against it. ... And it shall come to pass in **that day**, that I will seek to destroy all the nations that come against Jerusalem." - Zechariah 12:3, 9*

*"And his feet shall stand in that day upon the mount of Olives, which is before Jerusalem on the east, and the mount of Olives shall cleave in the midst thereof toward the east and toward the west, and there shall be a very great valley; and half of the mountain shall remove toward the north, and half of it toward the south. ... And it shall come to pass in **that day**, that the light shall not be clear, nor dark: ... And the LORD shall be king over all the earth: in that day shall there be one LORD, and his name one. ... And it shall come to pass in that day, that a great tumult from the LORD shall be*

among them; and they shall lay hold every one on the hand of his neighbour, and his hand shall rise up against the hand of his neighbour." - Zechariah 14:4, 6, 9, 13

21 Tribulation Overview

Let's take a look at some of the major events of the seven-year Tribulation. I have provided space below each entry for you to make notes pertaining to each event.

- Middle East Peace Treaty

  _____
  _____

- Jewish Temple construction begins

  _____
  _____

- Some economic prosperity during the first 3 ½ years as the Antichrist rises to complete control of the revived Islamic Caliphate

  _____
  _____

- Wars and rumors of war

  _____
  _____

- Famine

  _____
  _____

- Death by pandemic diseases

  _____
  _____

- Temple in Jerusalem commissioned

  _____

  _____

- Animal sacrifices in Temple begin

  _____

  _____

- Two witnesses/prophets appear in Jerusalem

  _____

  _____

- 144,000 sealed for Gods service

  _____

  _____

- Marked increase in Christian martyrdom

  _____

  _____

- Abomination of Desolation when Antichrist enters the Temple and declares himself god. This occurs in the middle of the seven-year Tribulation period.

  _____

  _____

- Lying signs ad wonders from the Antichrist and false prophet

  _____

  _____

- Mark of the Beast required

  _____

  _____

- Fire, hail and blood possible nuclear explosion

  _____

  _____

- Volcanic eruption causing severe air pollution and turning a large body of water red like blood

  _____

  _____

- Meteor striking the earth polluting fresh water supplies

  _____

  _____

- Sun, moon and stars smitten with partial darkness

  _____

  _____

- Demonic locust/scorpion like stinging creatures

  _____

  _____

- Large armies from the east move toward Jerusalem

  _____

  _____

- Nasty open sores on those that accept the mark of the beast

  _____

  _____

- The sea becomes as blood

  _____

  _____

- Fresh water rivers become as blood

  _____

  _____

- Intense heat from the sun

  _____

  _____

- Euphrates River dries up

  _____

  _____

- Global Earthquake

  _____

  _____

- Battle of Armageddon

  _____

  _____

- The Second Coming of Jesus Christ; the end of the seven-year Tribulation

  _____

  _____

22 The Millennial Reign

22.1 - 1000 Years of Peace

After Jesus Christ defeats the armies of Antichrist at the Battle of Armageddon, He establishes His Kingdom here on earth. Jesus will rule and reign from Jerusalem for one thousand years. This is commonly called the Millennial Reign of Christ.

"And I saw thrones, and they sat upon them, and judgment was given unto them: and [I saw] the souls of them that were beheaded for the witness of Jesus, and for the word of God, and which had not worshipped the beast, neither his image, neither had received [his] mark upon their foreheads, or in their hands; and **they lived and reigned with Christ a thousand years.***" - Revelation 20:4 KJV*

This will truly be a time of peace and prosperity for the planet. The death, destruction and pollution of earth, left in the wake of the Tribulation, will be cleaned up and disposed of. The Bible tells us that the angels will help in this cleanup as they remove everything from earth that offends the Lord Jesus Christ. The earth will be made clean and pristine, as it was in the Garden of Eden. How long this will take is not certain but I imagine it will happen fairly quickly.

"The Son of man shall send forth his angels, and they shall gather out of his kingdom all things that offend, and them which do iniquity; And shall cast them into a furnace of fire: there shall be wailing and gnashing of teeth." - Matthew 13:41-42 KJV

22.2 - Evil Expunged

All the offensive evil people will be removed from the planet and only the good will enter the Kingdom. Evil corrupt places will also be removed permanently. It will be almost heaven on earth. I say almost because Jesus will rule and reign with a rod of iron. Occasionally someone will step out of line and be on the receiving end of that rod. But by and large, everything will be wonderful beyond our belief and completely beautiful.

22.3 - Everyone Takes the Test

However, at the end of the one-thousand-year reign of Jesus Christ, the devil, Satan, is let out of the pit.

> *"And when the **thousand years are expired**, Satan shall be loosed out of his prison, And shall go out to **deceive the nations** which are in the four quarters of the earth, Gog and Magog, to **gather them together to battle**: the number of whom [is] as the sand of the sea. And they went up on the breadth of the earth, and compassed the camp of the saints about, and the beloved city: and **fire came down from God out of heaven, and devoured them**. And the **devil that deceived them was cast into the lake of fire** and brimstone, where the beast and the false prophet [are], and shall be tormented day and night for ever and ever." - Revelation 20:1-3, 7-10 KJV*

Wow, even when conditions on earth are perfect man still has a rebellious heart. Many are deceived into thinking they can throw off the rule and Lordship of Jesus Christ and take the planet for themselves. They are anarchists that love their sin and want to live in sin doing whatever their evil heart can imagine. Satan again deceives many people and gathers another great army. However, they have no chance of victory and are consumed by fire from the Lord God.

Why does this happen? Why is Satan loosed from the bottomless pit to deceive the world once more? Well, there are millions of people born

143

during the one-thousand-year reign of Jesus Christ. They have lived in a perfect world and not known evil as we have known it. They must be exposed and tempted by evil just like everyone else in ages past. During this time of temptation many are deceived and follow the devils lies. But they have no chance of success. They are destroyed and cast into the lake of fire, the final judgment for the wicked.

23 Great White Throne

23.1 - Judgment of the Lost

After the Millennial Reign of Jesus Christ and the final rebellion led by Satan is crushed, the Great White Throne judgment takes place. This is the judgment of the lost, the ungodly.

*"And I saw a **great white throne**, and him that sat on it, from whose face the earth and the heaven fled away; and there was found no place for them. **And I saw the dead, small and great, stand before God**; and the books were opened: and another book was opened, which is [the book] of life: and the dead were judged out of those things which were written in the books, according to their works." - Revelation 20:11-12*

At this point all the righteous people that believed in God and Jesus Christ the Son have been resurrected and are with the Lord on earth in His

Kingdom and in heaven. The only people that are still classified as dead are the lost dead, the unbelievers. They are all resurrected for the Great White Throne judgment to receive their sentence and to understand why judgment is upon them. This is the resurrection of the "unjust".

> *"And the sea gave up the dead which were in it; and death and hell delivered up the dead which were in them: and **they were judged every man according to their works**. And death and hell were cast into the lake of fire. **This is the second death**. And whosoever was not found written in the book of life was cast into **the lake of fire**." - Revelation 20:13-15*

It is not a good thing to stand before a Holy God and be judged according to your works. We are all sinners and made many mistakes, some intentional. We deserve the wrath of God but thanks be to the Lord Jesus Christ for His abundant grace and mercy to all that believe.

23.2 - The Second Death

The Book of Life is a book that contains the names of all true believers in the Lord Jesus Christ. Those whose names are not in that book are destined for the lake of fire for all eternity. This is called the "second death" as they will lose their resurrected body and die again thus being eternally separated from God, tormented in the lake of fire with the devil, the antichrist and the false prophet. All those that followed the Antichrist and all unbelievers throughout the ages will be there also.

24 New Jerusalem

24.1 - True Home of the Saints

The New Jerusalem is a huge city built by the Lord himself for those that believe in Him. Jesus said to his disciples:

> *"In my Father's house are many mansions: if [it were] not [so], I would have told you. **I go to prepare a place for you**. And if I go and prepare a place for you, I will come again, and receive you unto myself; that where I am, [there] ye may be also." - John 14:2-3*

The place Jesus is preparing is the New Jerusalem, the future home of all believers. This splendorous city descends from heaven and comes to rest on earth probably over the nation of Israel.

> *"And I John saw the holy city, **new Jerusalem**, coming down from God out of heaven, prepared as a bride adorned for her husband. ... And he carried me away in the spirit to a great and high mountain, and shewed me that great city, the holy Jerusalem, descending out of heaven from God, Having the glory of God: and her light [was] like unto a stone most precious, even like a jasper stone, clear as crystal;" - Revelation 21:2, 10-11*

The New Jerusalem is a magnificent city with streets of gold, gates of huge pearls and walls of precious gems. The proportions of the city are staggering. The city is 1500 miles on each side and has the same height. It could possibly be a pyramid structure but whatever the shape it will hold hundreds of millions of believers; a glorious home prepared for us by the Lord himself.

24.2 - Closing

I have included these last three chapters so you would have some idea of what was to follow the second coming of Jesus Christ. But your primary concern is keeping your faith in Jesus Christ no matter what happens during the seven-year Tribulation. Times are tough and getting worse, much worse. Keep your faith in Jesus and find some fellow believers. Avoid the Antichrist and his government forces as they will either imprison or kill you. Remember, Jesus is your testimony. Walk it out in faith and love.

Stand for Jesus regardless of the consequences. Whether you survive the seven-year Tribulation is not of primary importance. The important thing is that you spend eternity with the Lord and His saints. Stand in the strength and power of the Lord Jesus Christ, your reward awaits you.

"He which testifieth these things saith, Surely I come quickly. Amen. Even so, come, Lord Jesus. The grace of our Lord Jesus Christ [be] with you all. Amen." - *Revelation 22:20-22*

Pocket Guide to the Tribulation

Pocket Guide to the Tribulation